Word Builders: Using Vowel Teams to Build Big Words

Lucy Calkins, Series Editor

Havilah Jespersen, Elizabeth Franco, and Jennifer DeSutter

Photography by Peter Cunningham

Illustrations by Elizabeth Franco and Marjorie Martinelli

HEINEMANN ◆ Portsmouth, NH

For Roman & Quinn, may you grow up to be dream builders, and for Jeff, who is always on my team. —Liz

For Sanaa, who taught me that children are the foundation we build from.—Havilah

For Janice, Carolyn, Christina, and Lily, the strong and beautiful women who are always by my side.—Jen

Heinemann
361 Hanover Street
Portsmouth, NH 03801–3912
www.heinemann.com

Offices and agents throughout the world

© 2018 by Lucy Calkins, Havilah Jespersen, Elizabeth Franco, and Jennifer DeSutter

All rights reserved. No part of this book may be reproduced in any form or by any electronic or mechanical means, including information storage and retrieval systems, without permission in writing from the publisher, except by a reviewer, who may quote brief passages in a review, with the exception of reproducible pages, which are identified by the *Word Builders* copyright line and can be photocopied for classroom use only.

> *The authors have dedicated a great deal of time and effort to writing the content of this book, and their written expression is protected by copyright law. We respectfully ask that you do not adapt, reuse, or copy anything on third-party (whether for-profit or not-for-profit) lesson-sharing websites. As always, we're happy to answer any questions you may have.*
>
> —Heinemann Publishers

"Dedicated to Teachers" is a trademark of Greenwood Publishing Group, Inc.

The authors and publisher wish to thank those who have generously given permission to reprint borrowed material:

Tumbleweed Stew by Susan Stevens Crummel. © 2000 by Harcourt, Inc. Reprinted by permission of Houghton Mifflin Harcourt Publishing Company.

Cataloging-in-Publication data is on file with the Library of Congress.

ISBN-13: 978-0-325-10525-3

Editors: Karen Kawaguchi and Anna Gratz Cockerille
Production: Elizabeth Valway
Cover and interior designs: Jenny Jensen Greenleaf
Photography: Peter Cunningham
Illustrations: Elizabeth Franco, Marjorie Martinelli, and Kimberly Fox
Composition: Publishers' Design and Production Services, Inc.
Manufacturing: Steve Bernier

Printed in the United States of America on acid-free paper
22 21 20 19   VP   2 3 4 5

Acknowledgments

THIS BOOK WAS TRULY A TEAM EFFORT and we are so thankful for every single person who helped us build this unit of study. We certainly had a very big job to do and we are so lucky to have been supported by such a talented, knowledgeable, and generous crew.

First and foremost, we thank Lucy Calkins, who somehow sees what's not yet there. Thank you for envisioning this project, inviting us to become a part of it, and trusting us with a piece of this important work. You've seen our strengths and called us to act on them, and you've seen the places where we've needed to be shored up, finding us the perfect team to do just that. From you, we've also learned to see in whole new ways. You've taught us to reimagine, to redesign, and yes, to rewrite, so that these lessons serve the teachers and children who will bring them to life. Lucy, you inspire us as writers, as teachers, and as people. Thank you.

We are so very appreciative of Natalie Louis, who has led our work on this phonics project from the beginning. We thank you for your vision, your feedback, and your laughter. You helped us to the finish line!

Our colleagues at the Reading and Writing Project have been the foundation that allows us to reach new heights. We are so thankful for the years of research and collaboration that grounds our work. Thank you to: Amanda Hartman, Shanna Schwartz, Natalie Louis, Christine Holley, Sarah Picard Taylor, Celena Larkey, Rebecca Cronin, Rachel Rothman-Perkins, Allyse Bader, Angela Báez, Samantha Barrett, Emma Coufal Bemowski, Sara Berg, Nancy Brennan, Arlene Casimir-Siar, Lisa Hernandez Corcoran, Katrina Davino, Marjorie Martinelli, Kimberly Fox, Valerie Geschwind, Jessica Greiss, Lizzie Hetzer, Beth Hickey, Lisa Hourigan, Ann Keyser, Katherine Lindner, Sarah Mann, Casey Maxwell, Marie Mounteer, Nicole Santariga, Jessica Someck, Dani Sturtz, Cheryl Tyler, Elise Whitehouse, and Cynthia Williams. And to Lindsay Barton, our former colleague and co-author, whose work on *Readers Have Big Jobs to Do* helped shape this unit.

We'd also like to thank the leaders of the TCRWP, Lucy Calkins, Laurie Pessah, Mary Ehrenworth, Amanda Hartman, Emily Smith, and Audra Robb. Without you none of this would be possible.

We want to acknowledge that this book stands on the shoulders of so many brilliant minds in education and the teaching of phonics. In particular, it's been shaped by what we have learned from Donna Scanlon, Kimberly Anderson, and Joan Sweeney, as well as Isabel Beck and Mark Beck, Wiley Blevins, and Patricia Cunningham. Thank you for your contributions to this field of study.

We are extraordinarily fortunate to have had the wisdom, support, and generosity of Joe Yukish who took the time and energy to sift through our words. Thank you for clarifying, questioning, teaching, and encouraging us. Our work is better because of you.

A project this big requires so many parts. The artwork, the word cards, the charts, and all the rest proved to be a monumental effort. There is no one else who could have done the job as beautifully as Marjorie Martinelli. Thank you Marjorie for your extraordinary patience as we worked out all the tiny details and for being willing to make changes again, and again, and yes, (we're sorry) . . . just once more. You have made the tools used across this entire series shine. Thank you also to Kim Fox, Suzanne Korn, and Lisa Hernandez Corcoran, the artists who helped illustrate our words with so much color and joy. A special thank you goes to our youngest artist, Grace Báez, for helping us help other first graders.

A sincere word of thanks to the unparalleled team at Heinemann. Thanks to Elizabeth Valway for helping our words transform into a book we can hold and the countless hours it takes to make that happen. To Lisa Bingen and her team, we appreciate everything you do to get our work into the hands of teachers and the lives of children. And last, but not least, to Abby Heim who keeps the ship on course and does so with such skill and grace.

What a privilege to be teamed up with our fabulous editor, Karen Kawaguchi. We have been so lucky to work together on multiple projects and felt like a well-oiled machine as we jumped into writing this book with her by our side. Karen, thank you for your efficiency, your encouragement, and your ability to polish up our words so beautifully. We appreciate your support as we worked through the highs and lows (and heighs and hos) of writing this unit.

Thanks also to Peter Cunningham, thank you for the beautiful images of children that fill these pages.

For the extra bit of sparkle and joy in the final session of this book, we'd like to give a special shout out to Tanis MacMillian and her crew of first graders. They built their magical "Vowel Town" with such enthusiasm and happily shared their work with all of us. We know these photographs will bring smiles to our readers.

Finally, a special word of thanks to our closest crew members, our families, who know what it means to us to be able to add "writer" to the many titles in our lives and made space for this part of who we are. Thanks for letting us talk about vowel teams, when we know there are other things you'd rather be talking about. And thank you for sharing your Legos, your construction tools, and your stuffies so that our book can help other kids have fun, too.

With love and enormous thanks,
Havilah, Liz, and Jen

Contents

Acknowledgments • iii

An Orientation to the Unit • vii

BEND I We Are Word Builders: Using Vowel Teams that Make a Long-Vowel Sound

1. We Are Word Builders • 2

Today you'll teach students that it's their job to be a word builder—to learn the little parts that words are made of and use those parts to build new words.

2. Word Builders Pay Attention to Vowel Teams: Reviewing EE and EA • 10

Today you'll teach students to pay careful attention to what's in the middle of a word, especially vowel teams like EE and EA.

3. Digging Up Discoveries about Vowel Teams: An Inquiry • 16

Today you'll guide students to explore the inquiry question, "How do vowels work together to make a long sound?"

4. Word Builders Use Vowel Teams and Word Parts • 23

Today you'll teach students that word builders can use vowel teams such as OA, AI, and AY to help build words.

5. Watching Out for Words that Don't Work the Same Way • 30

Today you'll lead a shared reading session, helping students to discover that vowel teams do not always make a long vowel sound.

6. Word Builders Need Powerful Tools to Get the Job Done • 37

Today you'll teach students that word builders need tools to get the job done. You'll work with children to create a vowel team linking chart to use as a tool as they read and write words.

BEND II Building Words with Trickier Parts: Studying Vowel Teams that Make Two Sounds

7. Vowel Teams Can Make *New* Sounds: Learning the Vowel Team OU • 47

Today you'll teach students that some vowel teams work in special ways. You will introduce OU in a familiar snap word, out. *Then you'll demonstrate how OU works in the middle of words like* proud.

8. Using OU and OW to Learn New Snap Words • 53

Today you'll teach students there are two ways to make the /ou/ sound in a word, OU and OW.

9. Investigating the Sounds of OW and OU • 59

Today you'll guide students in an inquiry to see how the vowel team OW does different jobs in different words. You'll work with them to study sentences with OW words and figure out if the vowel team sounds like /ou/ in flower *or /ō/ in* know.

10. The Two Sounds of OO • 65

Today you'll teach students to distinguish between the two different OO sounds, /o͞o/ like moon *and /o͝o/ like* book.

11. Reviewing Vowel Teams to Build New Words: OU, OW, OO • 72

Today you'll remind students that there isn't just one way vowel teams work, so they'll need to try vowels in different ways when they read and write.

BEND III   Provisioning Our Toolboxes with Vowel Teams that Make the Same Sound

12. *OI* and *OY*: Two Vowel Teams, One Sound • 80

Today you'll teach students two new vowel teams, OI and OY, which both make the sound /oi/.

13. Helpful Clues for Vowel Teams *EW* and *UE* • 86

Today you'll teach students two new vowel teams, EW and UE, which usually make the same sound /o͞o/, like in the words stew *and* blue.

14. Word Builders Look Out and Listen Up to Use the Right Vowel Team • 93

Today you'll teach students to pay close attention to vowel teams because they can sound the same but look different.

15. Adding to Our Toolbox: Vowel Teams *AW* and *AU* • 98

Today you'll teach students that when they hear the /ô/ sound in a word, it's usually made by the vowel teams AW or AU.

16. Learning New Snap Words and Making New Words with *IGH* • 105

Today you'll teach students that letters can work in groups of three and the IGH team makes the long-vowel sound /ī/.

17. Building Vowel Town: A Celebration • 110

Today you'll help students celebrate all they've learned in this unit. Together, you'll build a map of Vowel Town, a place full of words with vowel teams.

 Registration instructions to access the digital resources that accompany this book may be found on p. xi.

An Orientation to the Unit

THIS UNIT IS GOING TO BE HARD WORK. Vowels may be one of the most complex parts in the English language. We're sure we're not the only ones who have cringed after coaching a child through decoding a word like *shouted*, only to watch them turn the page and run into the word *through* or *trouble*. Most vowels simply don't fit into tidy boxes or set rules. They are complex, working together as "teams" in complicated ways. It's the goal of this unit to help you and your students navigate this terrain in a practical way that supports the work children do as readers and writers.

If you're thinking about your students and worrying about how they'll be able to handle this hard work, don't be! Right from the start you'll see that this is a unit steeped in play, and we expect children will actually have a lot of fun taking on the challenge of learning more about vowels. "Let's go, let's go," you'll sing in the first session of this unit. "It's time to work. Let's go!" And then you'll send them off to take on the role of a *word builder*, using familiar word parts to build new words. Being a *word builder* then becomes the theme for the rest of this unit, as children learn more about vowel teams, one of the most important parts they need to read and write.

This concept of rising to the challenge of taking on big jobs and working hard will likely sound familiar to you if you've worked with the Units of Study for Teaching Reading and taught *Readers Have Big Jobs to Do: Fluency, Phonics, and Comprehension*. This phonics unit is designed to be taught alongside the reading unit and the two complement each other nicely. In particular, the work you do in this phonics unit will support the strategies you teach readers to use in Bend II of the reading unit, as they learn to tackle multisyllabic words by breaking them up and looking out for familiar word parts such as the vowel teams *EE* or *AI* and phonograms like *eed* and *ain*. Students will frequently bring their books to phonics workshop to try out some new work in the context of their independent reading. Tools from phonics workshop will get stored in children's book baggies, and your shared reading text from reading workshop will get used in whole new ways within phonics workshop.

Meanwhile, in writing workshop, we anticipate that many of you will be teaching "Music in Our Hearts: Writing Songs and Poetry" from the Grade 1 *If . . . Then . . . Curriculum: Assessment-Based Instruction* book. You'll see references to your writing work across this unit as children use what they know about vowel teams to edit class poems, take out their own writing to edit for the features they are learning, read poems searching for vowel teams, and sing songs reminding them of the jobs they are doing. We took every opportunity we could to make links between the work children are doing across phonics, reading, and writing.

It would be helpful for you to know that there are several goals to this unit and that this work builds off the previous units in this series:

- Develop a sense of flexibility when solving words with vowel teams, recognizing that:
  - some words have long-vowel sounds, represented by a vowel team
  - one vowel team can represent a number of different sounds
  - multiple vowel teams can sometimes represent the same sound
- Continue to develop a bank of high-frequency words that can be used to learn more about words.

Before describing the progression of each bend, it may also be helpful to clarify some of this unit's terminology. We use the term *vowel team* as a kid-friendly way of describing any group of letters that together represent a vowel sound. Used in this way, *vowel team* encompasses vowel digraphs that usually represent a long-vowel sound such as *EA*, *EE*, *AI*, *AY*, and *OA*. These are the focus of Bend I. It also covers digraphs that represent other sounds such as *OO*, *OU*, *OW* (the focus of Bend II), and *OI*, *OY*, *EW*, *UE*, *AW*, and *AU* (addressed in Bend III). This last bend will also include the trigraph *IGH*, teaching children that not just two, but three letters can team up to make a vowel sound.

You'll notice that the diphthongs *OU*, *OW*, *OI*, and *OY* are included in the list above. The term *diphthong* refers to the *sound* a vowel team makes. A *diphthong* starts as one vowel sound and moves to another. Try vocalizing the sound represented by the letters *OI*. You can feel your jaw moving. In contrast, your mouth stays still when you make the sound represented by the letters *EE*. While this is an interesting little fact for teachers, we don't feel that it's helpful for children to learn or use the term *diphthong* and we don't differentiate between these vowel teams and others when talking to kids. We aim to keep our language simple and clear when teaching children.

OVERVIEW OF THE UNIT

This unit is composed of three bends, or parts.

Bend I: We Are Word Builders: Using Vowel Teams that Make a Long-Vowel Sound

Bend II: Building Words with Trickier Parts: Studying Vowel Teams that Make Two Sounds

Bend III: Provisioning Our Toolboxes with Vowel Teams that Make the Same Sound

Bend I: We Are Word Builders

In Bend I, you'll launch this unit by introducing the theme of becoming word builders and then send your students off to do some actual building. Using snap cubes with word parts such as blends, digraphs, endings, and phonograms written on them, children will get to work constructing words, and challenge themselves to build longer, bigger words. Though it will take a little effort to initially prepare these materials, we've kept them as simple as possible and tried to envision ways you could do this using items commonly found in schools. You can find a detailed description of these materials in the Getting Ready section of this overview. The effort will be well worth the payoff in student engagement.

One theory as to why vowels tend to be so challenging for students is that they are commonly found in the middle of words (Beck and Beck 2013). Research tells us that struggling readers pay the most attention to the beginning of words, a little less attention to the ends of words, and the least attention to the middle, where vowel teams usually reside (McCandliss et al. 2003). To help your students understand the importance of looking carefully at the internal parts of words, you'll make a comparison to a construction project. "You'd never build a house with just a floor and a roof," you'll say. "And words work the same way. Word builders need to pay especially close attention to the middle of words where you find important parts like vowel teams."

This kick-starts your study of vowel teams. In this bend you'll first review *EE* and *EA*, which children learned in the second phonics unit, and then go on to study words with *AI*, *AY*, and *OA*. You'll notice that this collection of vowel teams usually represent long-vowel sounds. They're the vowel digraphs we think of when we hear the phrase, "When two vowels go walking, the first one does the talking." In reality this rule doesn't actually work very often, and your readers will notice this in many of the high-frequency words they see in their books such as *friend*. Donna Scanlon, Kimberly Anderson, and Joan Sweeney (2017) suggest that a more accurate version of this rule would be, "When two vowels go walking, somebody says something." Instead of teaching rules, it's more effective to encourage children to be flexible. Here's how this bend goes about doing that.

Early in the bend, your students will conduct a little inquiry, asking the question, "How do vowels work together to make a long sound?" By studying words like *wait* and *soap*, they'll discover that it's often the first vowel in a team that's making a long-vowel sound. But soon after this inquiry, you will highlight words such as *great*, which don't follow this pattern. We've learned from Donna Scanlon and colleagues that it's very helpful to teach children to see the vowels in words as decision points. "You are the boss of your reading," you'll remind kids. "When you run into vowels in a tricky word, it's decision time. You have to decide what vowel sounds to try, and think about what makes sense." Scanlon refers to this strategy as *vowel flexing*. To teach children to vowel flex, it can be helpful to give them a little order of operations. Teach them to first try the long sound of the first vowel, and then the short sound of the first vowel before doing the same with the second vowel. It's a surprisingly effective strategy and means that children don't necessarily need to remember all the possible sounds a vowel team can make. There are vowel teams we don't even cover in this unit such as *UI* and *IE* that can usually be decoded using the strategy of vowel flexing.

Alongside your teaching about vowel teams in this first bend, you'll also introduce a new set of high-frequency words. You'll teach four of these words (*wait*, *easy*, *away*, *each*) in an extension to the first session, layer in four more words in Session 4 (*near*, *need*, *next*, *last*), and finally teach the word *been* in Session 5. This may seem like a lot of words for your first-graders to master in a week, but keep in mind that most of these words contain a familiar vowel team and will connect to the teaching you are doing across the bend.

This first bend ends by introducing a tool used for the remainder of the unit—a vowel team linking chart. You'll place each of the vowel teams studied so far on the chart, along with an illustration and word to represent its most common sound(s). Instead of using a ready-made chart, we encourage you to co-create this with your students, letting them suggest what pictures they want to use and allowing them to participate in recording some of the information on the chart. In this way, it becomes another piece of interactive writing in your room and helps children to feel more ownership over the tool. This also makes it more likely that they'll use it all through their day, particularly in reading and writing workshop. This final session in Bend I acts as a mini-celebration for this bend, documenting the learning kids have done up to this point, and giving them a way to store and organize this new learning.

Bend II: Building Words with Trickier Parts

Bend II tackles a whole different group of vowel teams, ones that need to be explicitly taught. Unlike those taught in the first bend, these vowel teams (*OU*, *OW*, *OO*) can't be solved by vowel flexing and trying out the long and short sound of each vowel. Instead you'll teach students that these teams make a whole *new* sound that they'll need to remember. You'll also teach children that these particular vowel teams represent at least two different sounds, such as /o͝o/ in *book* and /o͞o/ in *school*. Your vowel team linking chart plays an especially important role in this bend. You'll want to keep it up to date and refer to it often so kids know where they can look to help them remember the sounds represented by these digraphs.

You may be wondering about the rationale behind teaching the vowel teams in this order. Diphthongs like *OU* and *OW* are considered more complex and in other phonics programs are often taught later in the vowel teams sequence. However, we found that these particular digraphs come up frequently in the texts first-grade children are reading. It therefore made more sense to teach them earlier in the unit to allow kids more time to consolidate their learning.

Bend III: Provisioning Our Toolboxes with Vowel Teams that Make the Same Sound

In Bend III, children learn about the less common vowel teams *OI*, *OY*, *EW*, *UE*, *AW*, and *AU*. These were grouped together because like the vowel teams taught in Bend II, these also need to be explicitly taught. Across the course of the bend, these vowel teams are taught in pairs that represent the same sound.

You may find that by the time you reach this third bend your students are fatiguing a little. You are covering a lot of material in this unit, at a fairly rapid pace. To help children rise to the challenge of this work, you'll generate some excitement by using your class mascot Rasheed. After doing some research about building and construction sites, Rasheed has decided to start drawing blueprints for a big project he's not quite ready to reveal to the class. Of course, this will pique your students' interest and they'll likely be quite keen to help him with whatever it is that he's planning. But there's a catch. Rasheed turns down their offer to help because they're just not ready. They need to learn *all* the vowel teams left on the vowel team linking chart before they can help him. We anticipate this challenge will put a little wind in children's sails when they most need it, spurring them on to learn several more vowel teams.

The unit then ends with a celebration where you'll reveal Rasheed's big plan to build not just a house or building, but a whole town made out of words—Vowel Town. In rug clubs, children will work together to decode and write words with vowel teams, working from a "blueprint" Rasheed makes for them. On a giant class map, they'll draw, label, and cut out items such as a *school*, *highway*, *restaurant*, and *playground*. You'll encourage your students to also add other buildings, objects, or signs, as long as everything on the map includes a vowel team. When children finish adding their drawings to the map you'll gather them one last time on the carpet to admire their project and remind them of how much they've accomplished with all their hard work.

GETTING READY

Rasheed the lion, our class mascot, plays an especially important role in this unit. He helps to build an engaging storyline by leaving your class to go off on an adventure to learn more about building, returning to share his learning and hear what your students have discovered in his absence, and then revealing your final celebration. You can, of course, use a mascot of your choice, but we do recommend playing along with the story of this unit as it's sure to keep children engaged and having fun.

In the first bend of the unit, your children will be physically building words by using snap cubes. We suspect that most schools already have a collection of Unifix® cubes that they use in math. Find a tub of these and using a marker, label them with a variety of different word parts. We recommend writing directly on the Unifix cubes with a wet erase marker. This way they can be easily cleaned off and returned to your math bin at the end of the first bend. However, several of the teachers that tried this work out said that they just chose to record the letters with a permanent marker. Another option would be to purchase small removable labels and stick one on each snap cube to write on. If Unifix cubes are hard for you to come by, it's also possible to use Lego® blocks, turning them so that they connect to build a horizontal word.

To distribute these snap cubes easily, we suggest using a plastic caddy with four different compartments. Label each compartment with one of the following categories: *Consonants* (this would include blends and consonant digraphs), *Vowels* (includes individual vowels and vowel teams), *Word Parts* (common phonograms), and *Endings*. Sort your snap cubes into the appropriate compartment and simply pass out one caddy to each group when needed. If you have enough cubes in a variety of colors, you might also choose to color-code the cubes in each section to make cleaning up easy to do.

We've determined the exact number of parts you need and designed the sessions so that you can use the same cubes for multiple sessions. Note that you will also be using snap cubes in your demonstrations and will therefore need to prepare a separate set of teacher materials. The following charts indicate the pieces you will need to label for each rug club as well as for your teaching demonstrations.

Session	Letter/Word Parts Needed for Each Rug Club
1	f, r, t, l, n, p, s, ch, sh, st e, u, ill, ay ing, ed, er
2	Add ee
4	Add ea, ai, oa

Session	Letter/Word Parts Needed for Teacher Demonstration (only 1 set needed)
1	st, an, d, ing ch, t
2	ea, b, t, ch, er, ing, s
4	t, oa, st, p, ai, n

Of course, if you don't have easy access to these materials, you can still do all of these word-building activities by having students write on individual whiteboards. In Bend II, your students will make the transition back to using whiteboards when "building" words. As in the previous units, this means you will need a class set of whiteboards with markers and erasers, as well a system in place to distribute these easily. On the other hand, if your students enjoyed using the snap cubes and you have enough cubes to continue this work in the next bend, you could absolutely do so.

In many of the sessions across this unit, you'll be looking at word cards to study the vowel team in each word and sorting words for vowel teams or phonograms. To simplify the prep work, you'll find most of these words available to print from the online resources (denoted with 👆) and as part of the Resource Pack (denoted with 📦). You'll want to make sure you have an easy way to display the words, and we recommend having a pocket chart in addition to your document camera and easel.

Your word wall continues to play an important role all through this unit. In each bend your students will learn a new collection of high-frequency words and add these to the word wall. You can find specific information as to what words are being added in each bend earlier in this orientation to the unit for Bend I and in the letter at the start of each bend for Bends II and III. These words will be available to print from the online resources, as well as in the Resource Pack. Your word wall acts as an important tool throughout many sessions, so be prepared to interact with it on a daily basis, highlighting features of key words, taking words off the wall temporarily to study them, and having students locate and use the words on display. You will want to make sure your word wall is located in a space that you and your students can access easily. At several points in this unit, you'll notice references to mini or individual word walls. These are available to print in the online resources. We recommend students keep a copy in their book baggies for reading workshop, as well as in their writing folders to use as a tool in writing workshop.

ONLINE DIGITAL RESOURCES

Resources that accompany this unit of study are available in the online resources, including all the charts, word cards, songs, and poems shown throughout *Word Builders*.

To access and download the digital resources for *Word Builders*:

1. Go to www.heinemann.com and click the link in the upper right to log in. (If you do not have an account yet, you will need to create one.)
2. Enter the following registration code in the box to register your product: UOSPH_JYAF9
3. Enter the security information requested.
4. Once you have registered your product it will appear in the list of My Online Resources.

(You may keep copies of these resources on up to six of your own computers or devices. By downloading the file, you acknowledge that they are for your individual or classroom use and that neither the resources nor the product code will be distributed or shared.)

We Are Word Builders: Using Vowel Teams that Make a Long-Vowel Sound

BEND I

SESSION 1

We Are Word Builders

GETTING READY

✔ Prepare a toolbox of Unifix cubes for each rug club. Fill each caddy with four kinds of word parts, including consonants (as well as blends and digraphs), vowels, phonograms, and word endings. Use a wet erase marker to label each cube with the parts: *f*, *r*, *t*, *l*, *n*, *p*, *s*, *ch*, *sh*, *st*, *e*, *u*, *ill*, *ay*, *ing*, *ed*, and *er*. You may decide to color-code each category to help distinguish parts. Refer to page 6 for a diagram.

✔ Be ready to use some Unifix cubes for your demonstration: *d*, *t*, *an*, *ch*, *st*, and *ing*.

✔ Familiarize yourself with the tune of "Heigh-Ho" from *Snow White and the Seven Dwarfs*. We've changed the lyrics but use this tune as a rally throughout the unit.

PHONICS INSTRUCTION
Phonological Awareness
- Segment single-syllable words.
- Change the beginning, ending, or middle phoneme to make a new word.

Phonics
- Identify blends, digraphs, common endings, and phonograms.

Word Knowledge/Solving
- Use known parts, including blends, digraphs, common phonograms, and endings, to build single- and multisyllabic words.
- Read words with inflectional endings.
- Decode unknown words using parts.

High-Frequency Words
- Learn four new high-frequency words: *easy*, *wait*, *away*, *each*.

IN THIS SESSION

TODAY YOU'LL teach students that it's their job to be a word builder—to learn the little parts that words are made of and use those parts to build new words.

TODAY YOUR STUDENTS will build words using letter- and word-part cubes—and also break down words.

MINILESSON

CONNECTION

Welcome students to the unit with a story about a construction site. Tell them that builders put little parts together to make something big, just as your students can put little parts together to make big words.

"Let's go, let's go. It's time to work. Let's go!" I sang softly to the tune of "Heigh-Ho" as students found their spots on the carpet. "This morning, I saw a crew of people working really hard to build a big, new office building. As I stopped to watch them, I realized something! That *big* building was actually made of lots of *little* parts, like boards and nails, cement and bricks, windows and doors . . .

"And every single person on that construction site had a really important job to do. They were all working to put those little parts together to build something *big*! For a minute, I felt like I was back in our classroom, because those builders reminded me a lot of you. You see, you are all builders, too, except instead of building offices, you build *words*."

❖ **Name the teaching point.**

"Today I want to teach you that you have a really important job to do in phonics workshop. It's your job to learn the little parts that words are made of and use those parts to build something big— longer words, longer sentences, and even longer stories! It's your job to be a word builder!"

WORD BUILDERS: USING VOWEL TEAMS TO BUILD BIG WORDS

TEACHING

Encourage students to suit up for the job of word building with imaginary construction gear. Channel them to talk in partnerships about the supplies they'll need to build words.

"We'd better get suited up for work before we start. Everybody, get your hard hats on!" I said, placing an imaginary hat on my head and smiling as I saw my class do the same. "Buckle up your tool belts! And don't forget your safety vests! Are we ready?

"Ready!" the class called back.

"Okay, now we need some materials. We need all the little parts that words are made up of. Turn and tell your partner what supplies we need to build some words." I gave children just a brief moment to whisper to their partners.

"I heard a lot of people say that we will definitely need . . ."

"Letters!" children filled in.

Share what you overheard about the materials the class will need to build words. Reveal a caddy of Unifix cubes, each compartment holding parts for word building, such as consonants and vowels.

"Right! We can't make a word without letters!" I held up a "toolbox" with four compartments containing labeled snap cubes. There was a section each for consonants (including blends and digraphs), vowels, endings, and common phonograms.

"This toolbox has lots of the little parts we'll need to start building. There are consonants," I said, pointing to that section of the caddy, "with letters like *R* and *P* and blends and digraphs." I held up a couple of the consonant cubes before pointing to the next section. "There are vowels. You know how important those are! Not just every word, but every syllable is going to need a vowel. And don't forget the difference one little silent *E* at can make at the end of a word," I said. "We are definitely going to need some vowels!" I continued pointing to the other compartments. "We'll need some endings like *-ing* or *-er*, and also some word parts like *ill* or *ay*—parts that we can find in a lot of different words. It looks like we have all the materials we need to start building!

"I've already pulled a bunch of these word-building cubes out of this toolbox. Will you take a look at the parts I have?" I set the toolbox down and placed my preselected cubes under the document camera.

To help organize these materials, you might consider color-coding each of the word parts, designating one snap cube color for consonants, including blends and digraphs, another color for vowels (and later, vowel teams), another color for phonograms, and a fourth color for endings.

Demonstrate how you build words, using a handful of word parts. Voice over to model your thinking as you try different ways the word parts could go together to make words.

"Let's see what words I can build with these materials." I placed my finger under each cube as I quickly named the parts.

"I know that blends and digraphs often come at the start of a word, so let's see if I can make a word that starts with *st*." I pulled the cube out. "Hmm, . . . I think I'm going to need a vowel next. I could use the vowel in the word part *an*." I snapped the two cubes together.

"*St . . . an*," I said quietly to myself. "*Stan!* That's a name! Cool. I just built a word! Let's see if I can add more to make an even longer word. I moved the letter *t* to the end. *Stan . . . t. Stant?* Nope. That's not a word." I pulled the letter *d* to the end. "*Stan . . . d. Stand!* That's a new word!" I snapped on the third cube.

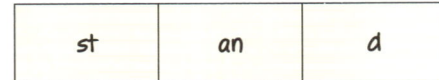

"And if I add *-ing* to the end, I get . . ."

"*Standing!*" the class shouted out as I snapped the final cube to the word.

"*Stand . . . ing*," I clapped. "Wow! I just built a two-syllable word using a bunch of little parts we already know."

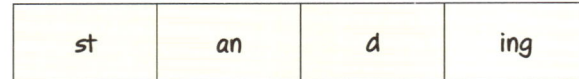

ACTIVE ENGAGEMENT/LINK

Set students up to build words with a partner. Suggest a word part for them to begin with and offer tips as they think about parts they could add on to make words.

"It's your turn now," I said, breaking the cubes apart and placing them back at the top of my work space. "This time, let's start with the word part /an/." I pulled the cube down. "Now talk to your partner.

What can you add to *an* to build a new word?"

"I'm hearing some of you say we could add a *d* to the end to build the word *and*, and some partners said we could add a *t* to the end to build *ant*! A little *ant* crawled across the grass," I said, adding some context. "Let's build it!"

FIG. 1–1 A teacher uses letter and word-part cubes to make the work of building words more concrete.

If some students find it challenging to imagine how these word parts might fit together without actually moving them, you might pass them a whiteboard to support their thinking.

"Now talk to your partner again. What parts can you add to build an even longer word? Remember, you could add to the beginning of the word or to the end of the word." The room filled with excited chatter as partners tackled this new problem. After a few moments, I drew their attention back to the cubes under the document camera.

"I heard Sonia suggest that we add *ch* to the beginning of this word. I snapped the cube on. Now this word says . . ."

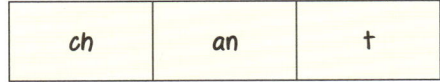

"*Chant!*" the class shouted out.

"Oh! What if we add *-ing* to the end?" I snapped the fourth cube on. "Now this word says . . ."

"*Chanting!*" a chorus of voices filled in.

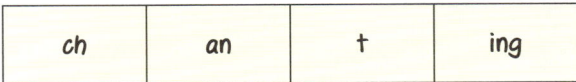

Use the word you built in a sentence and clap its syllables. Then remind students that little parts can fit together in lots of ways to build bigger words.

"Yes! *Chanting* . . . we were *chanting* the word wall words together. Or . . . She was *chanting* her favorite poem," I said, using the new word in a sentence. "Let's clap this word to count the syllables." We read the word again, clapping each part. "Wow. Another two-syllable word! These little parts can fit together in lots of ways to build bigger words! Nice job, word builders."

RUG TIME CLUBS

Organize students into rug clubs and distribute a toolbox for building words to each club. Coach students while they work together to build as many words as they can using their cubes.

"I have a toolbox for each rug club, filled with materials—word parts—that you can use to build your own words. First, gather some cubes. Then, just like I did, line them up to see what you have and get to work building! You can always grab more materials from your toolbox if you need them.

"Ready, word builders? Let's go, let's go. It's time to work. Let's go!" I sang aloud. I placed a plastic caddy of snap cubes in the middle of each small group.

If preparing these materials proves too difficult, know that this lesson (and the ones that follow across this first bend) will work using whiteboards and markers, instead. We use cubes as a way to engage students with making words, in a fun, new way, as well as to play up the theme of this unit. To modify today's rug time for whiteboards, you could create a shared "toolbox" on your easel, where you list some letters and word parts children can use to build words on their whiteboards.

If you have access to lots of snap cubes, you may decide to make duplicates of these letters so that each partnership can do this work. Otherwise encourage your rug clubs to work together. If your students need more structure, you could suggest taking turns building a word with the cubes while others record the same word on their whiteboard.

Then, I circulated around the meeting area as students worked, prompting as needed.

> ### POSSIBLE COACHING MOVES
>
> ▸ "Remember, every word needs a vowel. You'll want to make sure you have some vowel cubes or words parts with a vowel in them."
>
> ▸ "You chose -*ed*. Where does that part usually go in a word?"
>
> ▸ "Read it! Is that a real word? Try it in a sentence. If not, break it apart and try again."
>
> ▸ "See if you can add on another part to make an even longer word. You might try adding on to the end, or the beginning, or both!"
>
> ▸ "Are you missing a letter? You can use a blank cube to write the letter you need."

f, r, t, l, n, p, s, ch, sh, st	e, u
ill, ay	ing, ed, er

FIG. 1–2 To prepare for this bend, you'll want to include these parts in each rug club's "toolbox." You'll add a new part, or two, in later sessions.

SHARE • Word Demolition to Solve Long Words

Tell the class that word builders can do demolition to words, too. When they find long words in their reading, they can break them into smaller parts to solve them.

"We've been working hard to build words up, making them longer and longer. Now, how about we break those words down? Let's do a little demolition!" The kids jumped at the prospect. "Thumbs up if you've ever been reading along when all of a sudden—*bam!*—a big, long word stops you in your tracks. Me too! Well, whenever that happens, you can do a little demolition, jackhammering that big, long word into smaller parts you know. Let's try it together."

I pulled out one of the words we constructed with snap cubes, *standing*, and placed it under the document camera. "Let's pretend we got stuck on this word in our books. Let's practice breaking it into parts. Starting from the beginning of the word, we can look for parts we know. What's a part you see?"

"*S-T!*" several children called out.

"Yes, you might notice a blend at the start of a word. You can break that part off," I snapped off the first cube and left a space separating it from the rest of the word, "then you can keep moving across the word to look for other parts. What else do you see?"

I invited the class to call out suggestions and we quickly broke the word in a few different ways. First, we broke off the phonogram /an/. Then, snapping the parts back together, I quickly showed the class how they might instead see the word *and*. Then, we broke off the inflected ending.

You'll want to make sure kids are "demolishing" words moving from left to right. If you notice kids taking words apart in a random order or starting at the ends of words, coach them to start at the beginning just like you would when reading.

It's important to emphasize that that there isn't only one way to break up a word. Proficient readers are flexible in the way they break words apart.

I said, "We broke the word into smaller pieces. These parts work together to make a bigger word. Now let's build them back up to read the word. Ready?" One part at a time, I snapped the cubes back together as we crashed the word, *St-stand-standing*.

"Will you work in your rug club to do some demolition work with one of the words you built? Get out those jackhammers and break the word into smaller parts, then build it back up to read the whole word. Remember, you might break a word differently than your partners, so you can try it more than one way." I gave the clubs a minute to reverse their word building, breaking one of their words into smaller parts to offer some concrete practice with the word-solving work they do as readers.

As kids move through the hallway, observe the kinds of words and word parts they notice. Do they notice the beginnings and endings of words? Do they recognize common phonograms and vowel patterns? You might use this as a teaching opportunity and voice over what kids are noticing to the rest of your class.

EXTENSION 1 • Word Builders Notice How Words Are Built

Rally children to look closely at interesting words as they walk down the hall, noticing how words are put together and getting ideas for how to build their own words.

"One thing I know about builders is that they are always interested in other people's construction projects. They walk around, really noticing the way a house, office, or school is built. They admire the way it was put together, and notice all the interesting little parts, thinking, 'Hmm, . . . maybe I should try that when I'm building.'

"Did you know that word builders can do the same thing? Everywhere you go, you can be looking for words, noticing the way they are put together, admiring the little parts and thinking 'Hmm, . . . I could try that in my writing!' You might admire the way a little beginning or ending can change a word or spot a word part like *all*, which can help you make so many new words. You can learn so much by just being the kind of person that notices the interesting words around us.

"Let's try this right now as we walk down the hallway to the music room. Who knows what great ideas we'll get for our own word-building projects!"

EXTENSION 2 • Supporting Transfer to Writing Workshop— Writing Words Part by Part

Remind children to take the word-building skills they learn in phonics workshop and use them in writing workshop.

"Word builders . . ." I called out in the middle of writing workshop. Writers looked up from their pieces.

"Writers, I was just thinking about the construction site I walked by this morning. Those construction workers aren't just going to build that one office building and then never build again, they're going to head to a new construction site soon and start a new building. They will use their tools over and over again.

"Writers, it's your job to be just like those construction workers, building words not only in phonics workshop, but also during writing workshop. When you get to a word you want to write, you could say it out loud, listening for the parts, then build it part by part—except you won't use your cubes like we did today in phonics workshop. Instead you'll use your pen to write it, part by part."

EXTENSION 3 • Learning Four New Snap Words

 GETTING READY
- Before you teach, write a sentence for each new snap word on a sentence strip.
- Be ready to show the new set of snap words: *wait, easy, away, each*.
- Display the anchor chart, "Make it a SNAP word!"
- Prepare to distribute whiteboards and dry erase markers, one set per student.

Introduce four new snap words, and guide students through the process of making a word a snap word.

As kids gathered at the meeting area, I pointed to the word wall and said, "Word builders, are you ready for another challenge? Are you ready to build some new words?"

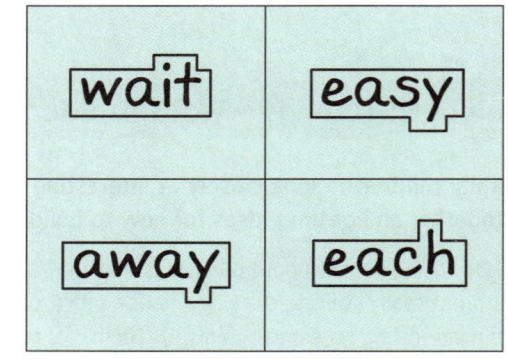

"Yes!" the class sang out.

"Get your word-building muscles ready because there are four new snap words to build and add to the word wall." I placed each new word card on the easel.

"Some of these words may already be snap words for some of you, and others will be new. Let's work so they're *all* snap words for everyone," I said, displaying the "Make it a SNAP word!" anchor chart.

I held up a sentence strip with the word *wait* underlined. "First, let's read our new snap word in a sentence."

I have to wait for the bus.

Then I held up a word card with the word *wait* in isolation. "This word says . . ."

"*Wait!*" the class filled in.

I placed the word card under the document camera. "Now, study it." I said, gesturing to the chart. "How many letters? Yes, four! Look closely at all the parts of this word. What are else are you noticing?" I paused for a moment to let students think.

8 WORD BUILDERS: USING VOWEL TEAMS TO BUILD BIG WORDS

"The first sound I hear when I say this word is /w/, *wait*. That's the *W*," I said, pointing under the first letter. Then I hear a long *A* sound. *Waaaaaait*. "That's the *A*," I said, pointing under the second letter. I then moved my finger to the letter *I*. "Hmm, . . . I don't hear a long *I* sound. Do you?" Students shook their heads as they quietly said the word to themselves. "That's interesting. It seems like the *A* and the *I* are teaming up to make that long *A* sound—it's looks like they're a vowel team! How cool. And the last sound I hear in the word *wait* is a /t/. That's the *T*."

We moved through the next three steps, then I added the word to the word wall before moving through the same process to learn each of the remaining words of the week. We made sure to make links between the new words and existing words on the word wall wherever possible, noting that the *EA* in *each* and *easy* remind us of *eat*, and the *AY* in *away* reminds us of *play*. At the end of the lesson, I reinforced using the word wall during writing workshop. "Whenever you need to spell these words, remember that they are here on the word wall. If you know it in a snap, write it quickly and use the word wall to check. But if you aren't sure, you can find it on the word wall, take a picture with your brain, then write and check!"

Your primary purpose here is to help kids learn to slow down and really study a word, noticing as much as they can about it. You'll especially want to emphasize the internal parts of words since these are often the hardest parts for young readers.

Don't worry too much about teaching into vowel teams right now. Simply noticing the A *and the* I *together is sufficient for today. You'll come back to this word in Session 3 to study it again and begin to make some generalizations about how vowel teams often work.*

SESSION 2

Word Builders Pay Attention to Vowel Teams

Reviewing EE and EA

GETTING READY

✔ Have a whistle on hand to get kids' attention to move to the rug.

✔ Be ready to use snap cubes labeled *ea*, *t*, *s*, *b*, *ch*, *er*, *ing* for your demonstration.

✔ Prepare copies, one per rug club, of a list of "secret words."

✔ Add a cube labeled *ee* to each of the rug club "toolboxes."

✔ Prepare word cards for: *eat*, *seat*, *beat*, *beach*, *teacher*, *teaching*, *see*, *free*, *seen*, *sheets*, *sheep*, *cheeping*, *set*, *bat*, *fell*, *test*.

✔ Prepare a pocket chart with *EA*, *EE*, and a blank header at the top of three columns to sort the word cards.

PHONICS INSTRUCTION

Phonological Awareness
- Distinguish the long- and short-vowel sounds in a spoken word.

Phonics
- Distinguish between two common long-vowel patterns, *EE* and *EA*, for the long *E* sound.
- Contrast short- and long-vowel sounds in words using common CVVC and CVC patterns.

Word Knowledge/Solving
- Use common long-vowel patterns *EE* and *EA* as well as digraphs and inflected endings to build new single- and multisyllabic words.
- Decode single- and multisyllabic words using common long-vowel patterns *EE* and *EA*, digraphs, and inflected endings.

High-Frequency Words
- Review and recognize snap words with automaticity.

IN THIS SESSION

TODAY YOU'LL teach students to pay careful attention to what's in the middle of a word, especially vowel teams like *EE* and *EA*. You will channel children to build new words using known high-frequency words and vowel teams, and also to break off and add word parts to make new words.

TODAY YOUR STUDENTS will review the vowel teams *EE* and *EA*. They'll build new words using snap words and vowel teams and also by breaking off and adding word parts.

MINILESSON

CONNECTION

Help children see that word builders need to pay attention to the middles of words, not just to beginnings and endings.

"Word builders, report for duty. To your rug spots!" I blew a whistle, ushering kids to the meeting area. Once the class had settled, I began.

"Yesterday, this classroom was transformed into a major construction zone! You were all hard at work putting little parts together to build *big* words. You snapped blends and digraphs to the beginnings of words and added parts like *-ing* to the endings of words.

"That is important work, but word builders can't just pay attention to beginnings and endings! You'll find that you need to work especially hard on the parts that come in the middle. Imagine someone building a house with just a floor and a roof!" The class giggled at the thought of a house with no middle.

"It would just collapse!" one voice called out.

"You're right, and the beginnings and endings of words would fall apart without a middle to hold them together. So, I have some important work orders. For the next part of our unit, let's make it our job to learn all that we can about parts you'll often find in the middles of words: vowel teams."

♣ Name the teaching point.

"Today I want to teach you that word builders pay careful attention to what's in the middle of a word. They especially watch out for vowel teams, like *EE* and *EA*."

TEACHING

Channel children to help you build new words using *eat* and to recognize the vowel team *EA* in the middle of words.

"Let's put on our hard hats and get to work. We have words to build!" I motioned as if fastening on a construction helmet, as kids played along. Then, I held up a snap cube on which I had written the vowel team *EA*. "Let's build words using this vowel team. We already know that we can add a *T* to the end . . ." I held up a second cube, on which I had written a *T*. Then, I snapped the cubes together, ". . . to build one of our snap words . . ."

"*Eat*!" the class shouted.

"Let's use this snap word to help us remember how vowel teams like *EA* work. Say it with me, *eeeeeeeeeeeat*." I slid my finger under the letters across the two cubes and stretched the word as the class joined in. "*Eat*. What vowel sound can you hear?"

They said the long *E* sound.

"Yes, I hear a long *E* sound, /eeeeeeeee/. The *E* and *A* are working together to make a long *E* sound.

"In the word *eat*, the vowel team is at the beginning of the word, so it's easy to spot. But what if we move it to the *middle* of a word? Can you figure out this next word I build?" I snapped an *S* to the start of the word.

Several voices called out, "*Seat*!"

"You got it, *seat*. Please sit in your own *seat*." Then, I slid my finger under the word to check the parts.

Research tells us that struggling readers pay the most attention to the beginning of words, and some attention to endings. However, they have a lot of difficulty looking carefully through the middle of a word (McCandliss et al. 2003). This becomes even more problematic when children encounter multisyllabic words in their books. These readers might say apring *for the word* appearing, *or* stemer *for* streamer. *In addition to self-correcting for meaning, it's important that children are explicitly taught to slow down and look carefully through the middle of a word, watching out for familiar parts.*

In today's session we remind children that the vowel team EA often has a long E sound. You'll notice we don't yet get into a discussion about one of the common patterns we see with some vowel teams—that the first vowel is the sound often heard in a word. This comes up in the next session.

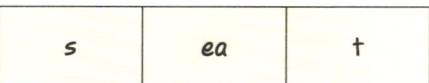

"Now, what if I demolish the first part of *seat* and add on a new beginning?" I pulled off the *S* and added a *B*.

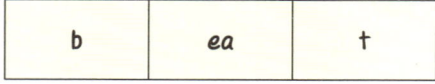

"*Beat*!" the class read in unison.

"*Beat*! We clapped our hands to the *beat* of the song." I offered a sentence to provide a bit of meaning to each word we built.

ACTIVE ENGAGEMENT/LINK

Ask children to help you break off and add word parts to make new words, continuing to use the *EA* vowel team in the middle of those words.

"Help me do a little demolition. If I wanted to turn *beat* into *beach*, what part do I need to change? Turn and tell your partner!" I listened a moment. "Yes, I hear you saying break off the *T*." I pulled off the *T*. "We need to change the ending *-t* to *-ch*. What letters do I need?" Kids called out the letters, as I snapped on a cube with the digraph, *CH*.

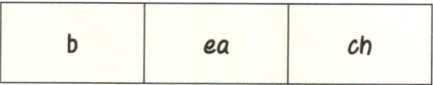

"Let's do a slow check. Do all the parts look right?" I slid my finger under the word as we read it aloud. "*Beach*! One hot summer day, we went swimming at the *beach*."

Then, we went on to build another two words, *teacher* and *teaching*.

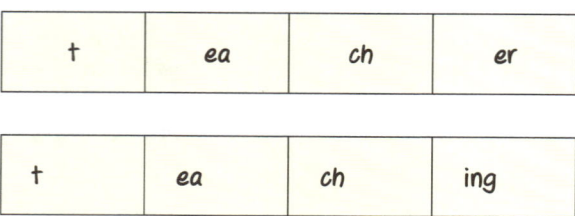

Here, the term "slow check" refers to the strategy of sliding your finger slowly under a word from beginning to end, checking that all the parts look right to confirm accuracy. This reading strategy is first taught in Learning About the World *from the Grade 1 Units of Study for Teaching Reading.*

RUG TIME CLUBS

Set up rug clubs to build "secret words" using cubes labeled with word parts.

"There's another vowel team you know that makes a long *E* sound, *EE*, like in *see*." I pointed to the word on the word wall. "Can you work together with your rug club to build some words with this vowel team in the middle?"

I distributed a plastic caddy to each rug club. "I am going to hand one job captain in each club a list of secret words. You'll be in charge of reading (but not showing) each word to your work crew. Job captains can supervise as the rest of the club works together to build the word. Then, the captain can do an inspection. Check to see if all the parts of the word are right and help your club fix it up if you need to. Then, read the next word on the list, build it, and check it. Off to work you go!"

I handed a list of words to one student in each club. Then, I listened in as students worked to build each word, coaching in as needed.

> ### POSSIBLE COACHING MOVES
> - "Job captains, look across the word, and use the vowel team in the middle to solve it."
> - "Does that make sense? Is that a word you know? Use it in a sentence."
> - "Word-building crew, decide what you need to do to turn *sheets* into *sheep*."
> - "Add the ending part you hear in *cheeping*."
> - "Job captains, do a slow check to make sure all the parts look right."
> - "Can you build any other words with EE using your cubes [*steep*, *feelings*, *cheered*]?"

SHARE • Sorting Words by *EA* and *EE* Vowel Teams

Invite students to read words, paying attention to vowel teams in the middle, and then sorting the words by vowel team. Alert kids that some words may not have a vowel team at all.

"I collected all the words we've built today on some cards. Let's read each word, paying careful attention to the vowel team in the middle. Let's put words with *EA* in one column of the pocket chart, and words with *EE* in another. But, watch out! I've also mixed in a few words that don't have a vowel team at all. It's your job to look across each word closely, paying extra attention to the parts in the *middle* to help us sort these words."

This activity will require your students to work together. You'll want to make sure all children are included and participating. If an individual is dominating a rug club you might want to make some modifications, perhaps suggesting each child take turns building the word while others coach them on. Alternatively, those not building the word with cubes could record each word on a whiteboard.

f, r, t, l, n, p, s, ch, sh, st	e, u, ee
ill, ay	ing, ed, er

FIG. 2–1 You'll introduce a new vowel team cube, *EE*, to each rug club's toolbox.

BUILDING WORDS...

1. free
2. seen
3. sheets
4. sheep
5. cheeping

FIG. 2–2 List of "secret words" to engage students in building words

I held up the first word card, *seat*, as kids read it aloud. Then, I pointed to the vowel team. "I see *EA* in *seat* and I hear /eeeeeeee/." We moved through the list in this manner, separating the *EA* words from the *EE* words, and making a third column for oddball words without a vowel team. Soon our pocket chart looked like this:

EA	EE	
eat	see	set
seat	free	bat
beat	seen	fell
beach	sheets	test
teacher	sheep	
teaching	cheeping	

"From now on, whenever you are reading or writing, you can make sure to pay attention to the middle of tough words. You can use vowel teams like *EE* and *EA* to help you read and spell words with long *E*."

When we sat down to write this book, it felt strange not to touch base with our friends at the SSDA. We've tucked this little note in here if you and your students feel the same way. Of course, if this storyline no longer resonates with your class, you can modify this letter to be from your principal or anyone in your school community. But we suspect children will be quite delighted to hear from these detectives.

EXTENSION 1 • A Challenge from the Super Secret Detective Agency: Find Words with *EE* or *EA* in Their Message

GETTING READY

- Display the letter from the SSDA to the class.

Read aloud a letter from the SSDA and challenge students to find all twelve words with *EE* or *EA*, paying special attention to the middles of words.

I stopped the class with a big announcement. "Oh my goodness, readers, you'll never guess who just sent us a message . . ." I held up a letter and said, "The Super Secret Detective Agency! Can you believe it? I wonder what they want to tell us. Let's find out," I placed the note under the document camera and read it aloud.

I turned back to the class, "That's right! You do know so much about the ways words work. You can use that knowledge to help you build and break bigger words. The SSDA must be keeping an eye on you. Let's read this message again and highlight all the words with *EE* and *EA*. We'll have to pay special attention to what's in the middle of these words. I think we need to be detectives for this job. Hard hats off! Detective caps on! Let's get to work!"

```
Detectives:

We hear you have some BIG new jobs.
Sometimes these jobs will feel hard,
so here's a little tip.
You need to remember
that you know A LOT about words.
Use snap words like see and eat
to help you remember vowel teams
that make a long E sound.
This will make reading and writing new words
seem easy!

Keep up the good work!


From: The SSDA


P.S. Say hi to Rasheed and your teacher.

P.P.S. Can you find all the words with EE or
EA hiding in this message?(Hint: There are
12!)
```

EXTENSION 2 • Word Builders Need to Know Lots of Words in a Snap!

GETTING READY
- Make sure your word wall is visible to all students.

Lead children in a choral read of high-frequency words on the word wall. Pause occasionally to have kids consider parts of those words that can help them spell other words.

"Our word wall has a lot of power! It has the power to help you get the job done when there's a big, long word in your books or when you need to spell a big, long word in your writing. These words have parts that can help you read and write *so* many more words.

"If you are going to be word builders, it's your job to know lots of words in a snap! Let's reread the collection of words on our word wall to make sure you will be ready to not only read and write those words, but also use them to build and break new words."

Together, I led the class in a choral read of our snap words. I pointed at one word after another as the students read down each list. Every few words, I stopped to nudge kids to consider the useful parts of a particular high-frequency word. "Oh! *Came* can help us spell lots of other words like . . . *flame*, *blame*, *tame* . . . this word part *ame* is really useful!"

SESSION 3

Digging Up Discoveries about Vowel Teams
An Inquiry

GETTING READY

- Print a copy of Rasheed's letter and hide the class mascot so the class can discover that he has gone on a trip.
- Display the words *eat*, *read*, and *wait* from the class word wall on an easel.
- Have ready magnetic letters to form and display vowel pairs *EA* and *AI*.
- Prepare a baggie of word cards, *reached*, *cleaned*, *brain*, *waist*, *afraid*, *boats*, *loading*, and *goal*, to hand out to each rug club.
- Prepare a list of *OA* words: *coat*, *throat*, *goats*, and *coaching* that you'll reveal in the share.

PHONICS INSTRUCTION

Phonics
- Identify common long-vowel patterns *EE*, *EA*, *AI*, and *OA*.

Word Knowledge/Solving
- Decode single- and multisyllabic words using common long-vowel patterns (*EE*, *EA*, *AI*, and *OA*) as well as digraphs, blends, and inflected endings.
- Use knowledge of CVVC patterns to decode new words.
- Read words with inflected endings.
- Use blends, digraphs, and phonograms to write new words.

High-Frequency Words
- Review and use snap words to build new words.

IN THIS SESSION

TODAY YOU'LL guide students to explore the inquiry question, "How do vowels work together to make a long sound?"

TODAY YOUR STUDENTS will explore how the vowel teams *EA*, *AI*, and *OA* work in words, gradually seeing patterns and drawing conclusions about those vowel teams.

MINILESSON

CONNECTION

Discover that the class mascot has gone on a trip, revealing a letter that asks the class to dig up more information about vowel teams.

I sat down in the meeting area, peering over shoulders and also scanning the classroom. "Class, have you seen Rasheed anywhere? I haven't seen him all day!" Students began searching from their rug spots.

"Wait, what's this?" I leaned over and pulled a folded note from the top of a nearby shelf. I opened it up and began skimming it. "It's from Rasheed! He says he's so excited about becoming a word builder he's gone off to learn more about building!"

I looked up from the letter and asked, "Where could he have gone?"

Kids called out guesses, "The library!" "The museum!" "A construction zone!" "Lego Land!" "College!"

WORD BUILDERS: USING VOWEL TEAMS TO BUILD BIG WORDS

I pressed on without brooding over any one guess. "Let's see what he has to say . . ." I read from the letter.

> Dear Builders,
>
> I am SO excited about becoming a word builder! I have decided to go out into the world to learn more about building!
>
> I have a job for you while I'm away. Can you dig up more information about the way vowel teams work?
>
> You'll have to teach me everything you discover when I get back.
>
> Your friend,
> Rasheed

"Wow! I can't wait to find out where Rasheed has gone and what he'll discover. Before he returns, let's get started on this big job. Let's dig up some dirt on vowel teams to discover how they make a long sound. Let's work together to answer this question."

 **Name the inquiry question.**

"How do vowels work together to make a long sound?"

TEACHING

Set students up to explore how vowel teams work in familiar snap words, *eat* and *read*, and begin to draw some conclusions.

"Okay, let's see what discoveries we can dig up. It helps to start with words we know. Let's study the vowels in these snap words." I pointed to the first word, *eat*. I slid my finger under the word as I read it aloud. "*Eat*. Hmm, . . . I see two vowels. Let's say the word again, this time let's stretch it and say it slowly so we can hear all the sounds." We read the word again slowly. "*Eeeeeeeeeeeat*. There's a long *E* sound in *eat*, but there isn't a silent *E* at the end of this word. What's going on here?" I paused for a moment, scratching my head, leaving a space for students to chime in.

You'll notice we start with the familiar, using a known word as well as a familiar vowel team to begin drawing conclusions about how vowels work in pairs. You'll use this to help students understand other vowel teams, like AI *and* OA.

SESSION 3: DIGGING UP DISCOVERIES ABOUT VOWEL TEAMS

Quickly the class pointed out the vowel team. "*E-A! E-A!*"

"Yes, that's right. We know that *E* and *A* can work together in a team to make the long *E* sound like in *eat* and *read*." I pointed to the word wall cards. "Hmm, . . . but let's dig a little deeper. Let's discover how this vowel team works.

"Take a closer look at this word. Work with a partner and say all the things you notice. Take a look at the letters. Listen to the sounds. Share what you're wondering." I gave students a few moments to study the word and share their ideas, as I listened in. Then I called the group back together.

"Many of you noticed that there are two vowels, first *E*, then *A*." I pointed to each letter. "And when you say the word *eat*, you can hear the /eeeeeee/. Do you hear the *A* making a sound? Let's listen for it . . . *eeeeeeeeat*." The students shook their heads, no. "No, I don't hear it either. I only hear the long *E*. It's like the *A* is silent.

"Does the word *read* work the same way?" I pointed to the second word wall card, pausing briefly to get kids thinking with me. "I see you nodding, yes. I see two vowels, *E* then *A*. This is how it sounds. *Reeeeeeeead*. I hear a long *E*, and I don't hear the *A* making a sound. So even though there are two vowels in words like *eat* and *read*, you only hear the *E*. Interesting."

You'll intentionally leave some room for discoveries, not perfectly defining the pattern seen in these vowel teams, so that students have some space to draw further conclusions.

ACTIVE ENGAGEMENT/LINK

Channel partners to explore vowel teams in the words *wait* and *plain* and to continue to figure out how vowel teams work.

"Will you and your partner study this next word, *wait*?" I pointed to the word on the easel. "Study the vowels in this word and listen to the sounds you hear. Then, see if you can dig up any new discoveries. Work together to come up with some more answers to our big question, "How do vowels work together to make a long sound?"

I prompted partners to get started, as I moved from pair to pair to listen in as the class deliberated. I said things like, "What vowels do you see in this word? What vowel sound do you hear? Which vowel comes first in that word? Is this vowel team, *AI*, working in similar ways to *EA*?"

These vowel digraphs may compel you to teach kids the rhyme, "When two vowels go walking, the first one does the talking." However, readers will quickly encounter words that don't follow this rule, and so we suggest that you keep your language tentative and encourage children to be flexible.

After a minute or two, I called the group back together. Then, I voiced back what I had heard. "I think we are on to something. You spotted the vowel team in this word, *A* and *I*. There are two vowels side by side. When you say the word *wait*, you can hear a long *A*, *waaaaaaaaait*. This time, the *I* is silent."

I pulled out magnetic letters to form each vowel pair. "So, in the vowel team *EA*, you hear a long *E* and the *A* is silent." I placed the two letters side by side on the easel. Then, below it I formed the next pair. "And in the vowel team *AI*, you can hear a long *A*, and the *I* is silent. Hmm, . . . are there any patterns developing here?" I left a bit of space to invite children to think along with me.

WORD BUILDERS: USING VOWEL TEAMS TO BUILD BIG WORDS

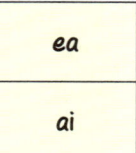

"The first one makes the sound," one voice called out. "The second vowel is always silent," another piped up.

"Wow! So, it seems that there are two vowels side by side in a vowel team, and the first vowel makes the long sound. The second vowel is silent.

"So, let's say you came across this word in a book." I wrote the word *plain* on a whiteboard. "Can you use what we've discovered about vowel teams to solve this word? Turn and read it with your partner. What vowel team do you see? What vowel sound do you hear? Does it follow the same pattern?"

I gave students a moment to check the word, testing out their theory. Then, I voiced over, "Many of you agree that this word works the same way! I see the vowel team *AI*. What's this word say?"

"*Plain*!"

"*Plaaaain*. Yes! I hear the long *A* and I don't hear the *I*. Job well done, readers. Studying words you know well, like *eat* and *read* and *wait*, helped you discover ways words work. You used the vowels in these words to learn more about how vowel teams can make a long sound. Together, we discovered that when vowels are side by side like *EA* or *AI*, the first vowel seems to make a long sound and the second vowel seems to be silent."

Of course, if your own students don't make these discoveries on their own, you'll want to help them recognize these patterns, as you study the vowel teams and name what you notice.

RUG TIME CLUBS

Rally rug clubs to continue to explore the inquiry question and study words with vowel teams *EA*, *AI*, and *OA*.

"Let's put this new knowledge to work right away! I have a baggie of words for each rug club. Look across the word from start to end and use what you discovered about vowel teams to help you read the word." I handed a baggie of eight printed words to each club, featuring familiar vowel teams, *EA* and *AI*, as well as words with a new vowel team, *OA*.

As children worked to read each word, I listened in and offered quick tips.

POSSIBLE COACHING MOVES

▶ "Start at the beginning to use parts you know. What's the first sound?"

▶ "Look out for vowel teams in the middle! What vowels do you see?"

▶ "Remember what we discovered about vowel teams. Try a long sound for the *A*. The *I* is silent."

▶ "Check the word. Does it make sense? Is that a word you know?"

▶ "Oh! That word has a new vowel team, *OA*! Use what you know about vowel teams to help you read it."

▶ "You solved the word *boats*. Does *OA* work the same way as *EA* and *AI*?"

SESSION 3: DIGGING UP DISCOVERIES ABOUT VOWEL TEAMS

SHARE • Discovering a New Vowel Team: OA

Guide children to study the vowel team *OA*, and figure out how the vowels work together to make a long *O* sound.

"I can't sneak a single thing past you! I tried to mix in some hard words with a new vowel team and you spotted those words and that vowel team, right away!" The class smiled proudly. I wrote the word *boats* on the easel. "What vowel team did you spot in this word?"

"*O-A!*" kids called out.

"Yes, right here in the middle of the word." I pointed under the vowels. "Hmm, . . . does *OA* work the same way as *EA* and *AI*? Does it make a long *O* sound? Let's check." I slid my finger under the word. "B/ot/s?" I made a short-vowel sound then demonstrated cross-checking for meaning. "Bots? Does that make sense?"

"Noooo!!!"

"The short sound doesn't work. Let's try the long vowel. *Booooats*. *Boats*! Yes, that's a word I know! The *O* is making a long sound and the *A* is silent."

I quickly wrote the letters *OA* on the easel, under the word *boats*. "Say /ō/ when I point to this vowel team," I said, pointing under the letters *OA*. "Now let's read this word again." I ran my finger under the word *boats* as the class read the word together.

> boats
>
> oa

"Let's use what we know about this vowel team to read some more words. Ready?"

I unveiled a list of new words with the vowel team *OA*, including *coat, throat, goats, and coaching*. We worked together to read them.

When introducing vowel teams, Beck and Beck (2013) recommend first exposing children to the concept within a word (e.g., boats*), then looking at the vowel team in isolation (writing* OA *and reading it) and then moving back to using that part within a word. You will notice we follow this sequence here and throughout many sessions in this unit.*

EXTENSION 1 • Word Builders Use Notebooks, Too!

GETTING READY

- Make sure children have the notebooks they used as word detectives from the second phonics unit.
- Your name chart, word wall, charts, and agenda should be visible to all your students.

Invite children to be on the lookout for words with vowel teams—and keep a collection of these words in their notebooks.

"Remember the little notebooks you were using to help you be a word detective? Well, guess what? A word detective is not the *only* person who uses a notebook. Word builders can use notebooks, too! Instead of jotting down clues to solve a mystery, like a detective would, word builders use a notebook to jot down information they want to remember for their future construction projects. They are always on the lookout for materials they find helpful or ideas they don't want to forget.

FIG. 3–1 Collecting words with vowel teams in a "Word Builder Notebook."

"You may have tucked your notebook away, after solving all the cases as word detectives, but now it's time to take that notebook out and put it to good use. Take a moment to find your handy-dandy notebook. It can't have gone far!" Kids quickly looked in book baggies and writing folders for the notebooks they used as word detectives and put them on their table.

"Let's try using these notebooks right now as word builders. Today you discovered some new vowel teams, *AI* and *OA*, and I bet those teams don't just exist in the words you studied during phonics workshop. I bet they exist everywhere.

"Flip to a new page and grab a pen." I paused as kids readied their notebooks in anticipation. "Start studying the words all across the room. You could look at the name chart, word wall, the charts, and agenda. When you notice a word with a vowel team, jot it down. You may even want to work with another word builder. Tell them what you are noticing and why you are writing it down. You can even trade words the way builders trade tools and ideas."

EXTENSION 2 • Snap Words Have Building Power

 GETTING READY

- Hand out whiteboards and a marker to each partnership.

Channel partners to use the word wall as a tool to help them build new words.

"Word builders, meet me near the word wall with your partner." As kids gathered close I handed out one whiteboard and one dry erase marker to each partnership. "It's important for a construction crew to know how to use lots of different tools, because you never know what tools you might need to get the job done. The same thing is true for word builders. It's important to know how to use all your tools to build new words. One very important tool for building new words is the . . ."

"Word wall," the class cheered, as I pointed behind me.

"Just like word parts such as vowel teams and endings can help you build new words, snap words can help you build new words, too. If you know the word *think*," I pointed to the word on the word wall, "you can build lots of new words such as *wink* or *blink* or . . ." Kids chimed in with other words such as *pink* and *sink*.

Invite partners to play a game. Point to a word wall word, then partners can build as many new words as they can with that word.

"Let's keep the building power of snap words going by playing a little game. I'll point to a word on the word wall and you and your partner work together to build as many new words as you can. Remember, you can keep the vowel or vowels and the ending of the word, like the *-ink* in *think*, to help you build new words. Just switch the beginning letters or parts to make new words.

"Partner 1, take the dry erase board and marker. Get ready to record. Partner 2, get ready to think. Your first word is *each*." Partners started building words like *beach*, *teach*, and *reach*. I reminded them to not forget blends and digraphs as they continued to build.

We continued the game with a few more words from the word wall such as *make* and *see*.

You may want to display or provide kids with a copy of the ABC or "Blends and Digraphs" chart to support them to make new words.

FIG. 3–2   Using snap words to write more words.

22

WORD BUILDERS: USING VOWEL TEAMS TO BUILD BIG WORDS

SESSION 4

Word Builders Use Vowel Teams and Word Parts

IN THIS SESSION

TODAY YOU'LL teach students that word builders can use vowel teams such as *OA*, *AI*, and *AY* to help build words. You will work with kids to build the words *toast* and *paint*, listening for the beginning and ending sounds and the vowel sounds in the middle to help identify the vowel team. Then you'll set up rug clubs to build their own words.

TODAY YOUR STUDENTS will build words with the vowel teams they've learned so far to consolidate their learning. Expect them to use their phonics tools: saying words slowly, listening for all the parts, identifying letter sounds, looking for vowel teams, and doing a slow check after they build the words.

GETTING READY

✓ Be ready to use cubes labeled *t, oa, st, p, ai,* and *n* for your demonstration.

✓ Display a page of Rasheed's drawings of *toast, paint, sleep, feet, leaf, chain, train,* and *soap*. Also prepare copies of this sheet for each rug club.

✓ Add the vowel teams *EA*, *OA*, and *AI* to each rug club's toolbox. See Fig. 4–1 for reference.

MINILESSON

CONNECTION

Tell children that Rasheed has sent some pictures and needs help building the words. Remind kids that they can use all the word parts they know—letters, blends, digraphs, endings, and vowel teams.

"Word builders, put on your hard hats and tool belts and meet me at the rug, I have some news to share." Kids gathered quickly, excited to hear what I had to say.

"Early this morning, while I was getting ready for you to arrive, my phone rang. It was Rasheed! I could barely hear him! There was *so* much noise in the background . . . banging and buzzing and blasting and crashing!" I said, hinting at his whereabouts. "He called to check in and asked if you've been busy learning more about vowel teams. I told him you'll have lots to teach him when he returns.

"Then, he told me he needs our help. He has lots of words he wants to build, but he isn't sure what parts he needs to use, so he just drew the pictures. He emailed them to me and I've printed out copies for us. Will you help him use the right letters and word parts to build these words?"

PHONICS INSTRUCTION

Concepts About Print
- Use proper language conventions to write a sentence, including capitals and end punctuation.

Phonological Awareness
- Isolate and pronounce initial, medial vowel, and ending sounds in spoken single-syllable words.

Phonics
- Identify common long-vowel patterns *EE*, *EA*, *AI*, and *OA*.
- Distinguish between two vowel patterns that make the same sound: *AI* and *AY*.
- Recognize and use some phonograms with vowel combinations (*-ail*, *-ain*).

Word Knowledge/Solving
- Use knowledge of common long-vowel patterns (*EE*, *EA*, *AI*, and *OA*) as well as digraphs, blends, and inflected endings to build single- and multisyllabic words.
- Use knowledge of CVVC patterns to decode new words.

High-Frequency Words
- Learn new words: *near, need, next,* and *last*.

"Yes!" kids chimed back.

"Well, if we are going to get this job done, you'll need to remember to use all the words and parts you know, like blends and digraphs, and endings. Oh! Don't forget vowel teams!"

♣ Name the teaching point.

"Today I want to teach you that word builders can use vowel teams to help build words. When you hear a long-vowel sound in the middle of a word, you can stop and think, 'Would a vowel team help me build this word?'"

TEACHING

Demonstrate building the word *toast*: listen for the beginning letter sound, stretch out the word to hear the vowel sound in the middle, and listen for the ending letter sounds.

"Let's get building! First, I need to make sure I have all the tools I need. Blends and digraphs, endings, oh yes, and vowel teams," I said out loud as I placed my cubes under the document camera. "Hmm, . . . it seems like Rasheed needs some help building . . ." I let my voice trail off as I pointed to the first picture on the page of drawings.

"*Toast*!" the class chimed in.

"Let me say this word slowly, hear all the parts, and think about what I need to build this word. Say it along with me. *Tooooast*. I hear /t/ at the beginning," I said as I fished a letter *t* out of the caddy.

"What's the next sound you hear?" I stretched the word again and emphasized the long *O* sound as the class joined in.

"Oooooo," kids replied, stretching the long *O* sound.

"Yes, I hear a long-vowel sound, /ō/. Wait! I think we can put a vowel team to work. *OA* makes the long *O* sound," I said as I snapped the *OA* vowel team cube next to the letter *T*. "And I hear the sound /st/ at the end," I said as I finished building the word. Then I slid my finger under the word to check all the parts.

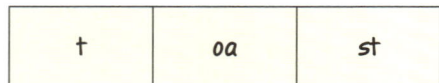

"Vowel teams can sure come in handy when you're building words and you hear a long-vowel sound."

ACTIVE ENGAGEMENT/LINK

Work with children to build the word *paint*, listening to letter sounds, stretching out the word, and identifying the vowel team, *AI*.

"Let's look at another picture Rasheed sent." I pointed to the second picture on the printed page.

"*Paint*. Let's stretch it and listen for the parts we hear." We said the word slowly together. "*Paaaaint*."

"What sound do you hear at the beginning? What letter do we need?" I quickly pulled the *P* from the pile of cubes. "What next? Stretch the word again with your partner and decide what goes in the middle of the word *paint*." I gave partners a moment to talk, before voicing over.

"I'm hearing you say you hear a long *A* sound in *paint*, *paaaaaaint*. Yes, I hear it, too. You know one way to change the vowel to a long sound is with a silent *E*, but in this word, we need a vowel team to make that sound. What vowel team can we use to make a long *A* sound?" I invited the class to chime in as I built the word with snap cubes. Then, I quickly recruited the kids to help me add the ending.

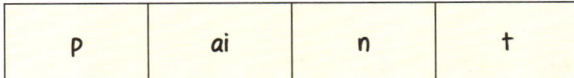

I ran my finger underneath the cubes and checked the parts along with the kids. "*Paaaaaaint*. You heard the long *A* in the middle of the word, *paint*, so you remembered to use a vowel team. *AI* works together to make the long *A* sound."

RUG TIME CLUBS

Set up rug clubs to build words by studying pictures and using their phonics tools.

"Word builders, I think you have what it takes to finish this job. I am going to hand each club a copy of Rasheed's pictures. Use your tools to build these words with your club.

"Remember to look at the picture together and say the word slowly, listening for all the parts. If you hear a long vowel in the middle, don't forget that your vowel teams can help get the job done. After you build the word, do a slow check. Then write that word under the picture so you can give those words back to Rasheed. Then, build the next word."

I handed out caddies now containing the additional vowel teams *EA*, *OA*, and *AI* along with copies of the sheet of pictures.

f, r, t, l, n, p, s, ch, sh, st	e, u, ee, ea, oa, ai
ill, ay	ing, ed, er

FIG. 4–1 You'll introduce new vowel team cubes to each rug club's toolbox including *EA*, *AI*, and *OA*.

As children worked to solve each word, I listened in and offered quick tips.

> **POSSIBLE COACHING MOVES**
>
> ▶ "Start at the beginning to use parts you know. What's the first sound?"
>
> ▶ "Listen for the vowel sound in the middle! What vowel team could help you?"
>
> ▶ "Don't forget to listen at the end of the word."
>
> ▶ "Check the word. Do a slow check. Do you have all the parts? Do they look right?"
>
> ▶ "Remember that the long *E* sound could be the vowel teams *EE* and *EA*, you might need to try it two ways."

Your students may not have time to build all of these words, and you'll want to bring this work to a close when your time is up. However, there should be enough words here to keep children problem solving and working productively for the duration of your rug time.

SHARE • Spelling with a Familiar Vowel Team, AY

Remind students that they can build words with long *A* sounds with a silent *E* or with vowel teams *AI* or *AY*. Work with them to build the words *spray* and *rain*.

"Word builders, I have an important reminder. Listen up. When you build words with a long *A* sound, you know you might need to use a silent *E* at the end, like in *cake*, or a vowel team, *AI* like in *train*." I quickly wrote the examples on a whiteboard.

"But, that's not the only way *A* can make a long sound! Don't forget about *AY*, like at the end of our snap words *play* and *away*," I wrote the words on the whiteboard, pointing to the end of each word. "*A* and *Y* work a lot like *A* and *I*. So, how will we know when to use one vowel team and not the other?

"Here's a helpful tip. *AY* is usually found at the end of a word. So, when you are writing and you hear long *A* in the middle, you can use a silent *E* or the vowel team *AI*. When you hear long *A* at the very end of a word, try *AY*. Then, you can check to make sure the word looks right.

"Let's try it. Let's write the word . . . *spray*! Don't *spray* me with water!" I quickly wrote the first part of the word on the easel. Then, I stretched the word to isolate the vowel sound. "*Spr-ayyyyy*. Do you hear the long *A* sound in the middle of the word or at the end?" The class responded that they heard the vowel at the end. "I agree. I hear /ā/ at the very end of *spray*. That means we can use *AY* to write it." I filled in the last part of the word, then slid my finger under the whole word to check it. "*Spr-ayyyy*. That looks right!

If you have a Maya, Payton, or Layla in your room, they'll be sure to point out that AY isn't always found at the end of a word. Names provide many of the exceptions to this generalization. You'll notice that once again we use tentative language here. The AY combination is usually found at the end of a word. You'll want to make sure you don't present phonics principles as absolutes or rules. If kids notice exceptions, make note of them and celebrate the close looking it takes to discover these words.

"Now let's try it with the word, *rain*. I hope it doesn't *rain* during our picnic. Say the word slowly and listen for the long *A* sound. Do you hear it in the middle or at the end?"

"Middle!" several voices answered.

"*Rainnnnnnn*. Yes, I hear long /aaaaaaaa/ in the middle, too. I hear /nnnnn/ at the end of the word. Talk with your partner. What part can we use to write the long *A* sound in *rain*?"

After a few moments, I called the class back together. "Some of you are thinking we could use a silent *E* and some of you are thinking we should use the vowel team *AI*. Let's try it both ways and check to see which looks right." I quickly wrote *rane* and *rain* on the easel and we concluded that *rain* was spelled correctly. I circled it, modeling the process I hoped writers would use when problem solving the spelling of new words. Then, I quickly reminded the children to keep this tip in mind when they are working hard to spell words during writing workshop.

EXTENSION 1 • More Practice with the Phonograms *-ail* and *-ain*

GETTING READY
- Have ready chart paper and marker to make a two-column chart.
- Have students bring their whiteboards and dry erase markers to the carpet.
- Display the class ABC and "Blends and Digraphs" charts nearby.

"Today we figured out how to spell the word *rain*. It has the pattern *A-I-N* at the end. There are actually a lot of words that use this pattern." I wrote the pattern *-ain* on the top of a sheet of chart paper with the word *rain* under it. "And there's also another pattern with the vowel team *AI* that you'll see in many words in your books. It's *A-I-L*, like in *snail*." I wrote this second pattern on the other side of the chart paper with the word *snail* underneath. "These two patterns can be so helpful in your reading and writing.

"Will you see if you can think of other words that have these patterns? Work with your partner and build these words by making a list on your whiteboard. Pick one of these patterns to start. Then try adding some letters to the start or the end and see how many words you can come up with. You can use our class ABC and 'Blends and Digraphs' charts to help you, too! Keep the words on your board so you can share them with the class when we're done. Off to work you go!"

I circulated around the group while children worked, building words like *train*, *pain*, *sprain*, *tail*, *failed*, and *email*. Children then shared their words as I recorded them on chart paper. We read through the list of words together as a class.

The phonograms -ail and -ain are two of the thirty-seven most common phonograms that can be used to make nearly 500 different words (Wiley and Durrell, 1970). Spending a little extra time working on these will be beneficial for your readers and writers since you can expect they will encounter words with these patterns regularly.

EXTENSION 2 • Giving Directions on a Construction Site: Adding New High-Frequency Words to the Word Wall

GETTING READY

- Be ready to display word cards for new high-frequency words, *near*, *need*, *next*, and *last* and add them to the word wall.
- Display the anchor chart, "Make it a SNAP word!"

Rally children to make the words *last*, *next*, *need*, and *near* into snap words by using familiar steps.

I stood in the middle of the room and called out some directions to kids, with an emphasis on the word wall words I was about to teach. "The *last* person to enter the room needs to shut the door. Writing workshop is *next* on our daily schedule—you *need* to get your folders out! Please sit *near* your partner!"

The kids giggled and gave me a funny look. I smiled back and said, "I was just trying to get my construction crew in order," as I pointed from student to student. "I walked by the construction site again today and noticed that workers on the crew were giving each other a lot of directions. These directions seemed to help everyone know what to do. As I stopped and listened carefully, I recognized that the crew was using words we sometimes use to give directions, words such as *last*, *next*, *need*, and *near*." I held up a card with each of these words written down. "I thought these words could be helpful to add to the word wall. They are also words I know you see often in your books and use when you write.

"These words could be ones you already know how to read and write in a snap, but before adding these new words to the wall, let's practice them using the 'Make it a SNAP word!' chart." As each student grabbed a whiteboard and dry erase marker, I placed the snap word chart and the new words on the easel.

Together, we went through each step before adding the four words to the class word wall.

EXTENSION 3 • Assessing CVVC Knowledge: Applying the CVVC Principle to Write a Sentence

Use a dictated sentence to conduct a quick assessment of the CVVC principle.

"Word builders, I can tell that your skills are already getting stronger. Let's take a minute to show off these skills and everything you know about using vowel teams in the middle of words. I'm going to tell you a few sentences from a story I'm writing, and your job is to listen closely, and then figure out how to write down what I say. The story is about playing at my friend's house. I'm going to say it once quickly, and then say it again slowly so that you have time to write down each word. Ready?

"We played with his sailboat, his frisbee, and some clay. Then we had treats."

I then repeated the sentences slowly, pausing between each word to give students a chance to write it down. "Write it the best you can," I encouraged, making sure their work would accurately reflect what they were able to do with independence. I gave them a moment to check their work and then collected the papers to analyze later.

Take some time to analyze the work your students did during this dictation to plan possible small groups. Make note of students who miss or confuse vowel teams. You may also note students who used the CVCe pattern in place of vowel teams to spell words. You might pull these children together in a small group during writing workshop, for more practice listening to the sounds they hear and using the linking chart.

SESSION 5

Watching Out for Words that Don't Work the Same Way

GETTING READY

✓ Display the "Greetings from New York City!" postcard from Rasheed along with a photograph of the lion at a construction site. Be ready to hand out copies of the text to partners during rug time.

✓ Have pens for each partnership.

✓ Have a sheet of chart paper on an easel and some markers for interactive writing.

PHONICS INSTRUCTION

Phonological Awareness
- Isolate and pronounce initial, medial vowel, and ending sounds in spoken single-syllable words.

Phonics
- Identify common long-vowel patterns *EE*, *EA*, *AI*, *AY*, and *OA*.
- Distinguish between two vowel patterns that make the same sound: *EE* and *EA*.

Word Knowledge/Solving
- Identify and read words with inconsistent but common spelling-sound correspondences.
- Use knowledge of long-vowel CVVC patterns to decode new words.
- Use knowledge of common long-vowel patterns (*EE*, *EA*, *AI*, and *OA*), as well as digraphs, blends, and inflected endings to write words.

High-Frequency Words
- Learn one new word: *been*.
- Spell snap words with automaticity.

IN THIS SESSION

TODAY YOU'LL lead a shared reading session, helping students to discover that vowel teams do not always make a long vowel sound.

TODAY YOUR STUDENTS will use all they know about solving words and their knowledge of vowel teams to read and write.

MINILESSON

CONNECTION

Invite children to sing "Be a Reading Boss."

As kids gathered in their rug spots, I hummed to myself, then sang a few lyrics, just loud enough for kids to hear, "If you think something's wrong, you've got to stop . . . If you think something's wrong, you've got to stop . . ." Then I said, "Readers, I just can't get our 'Be a Reading Boss' song out of my head! I've been singing it all week! Will you sing the last verse with me?" I began as the students joined in:

Be a Reading Boss

(To the tune of 'If You're Happy and You Know It")

Be the boss of your reading, be the boss!
Be the boss of your reading, be the boss!
When the job gets really tough,
And you want to huff and puff . . .
Be the boss of your reading, be the boss!

"That's an important message. You need to be the boss of your reading, especially when that job gets really tough! And one thing that can make the job of reading feel tough is finding vowel teams in the words you're trying to figure out."

❖ **Name the teaching point.**

"Today I want to teach you that reading bosses make decisions! Whenever you spot a vowel team in a tough word, it's decision time! You might have to try the vowel sound a few different ways, listening for a word that makes sense and sounds right."

TEACHING AND ACTIVE ENGAGEMENT/LINK

Invite the class to join you in a shared reading of a postcard from Rasheed, using their knowledge of vowel teams to figure out words like *greetings, been, nearly, street, learn, roads,* **and** *train.*

"This reminder came at the perfect time because I have something very special for us to read together right now!" I held up a postcard. "A postcard arrived today . . . from Rasheed! He sent a photograph, too! Look!" I showed the class.

FIG. 5–1   Rasheed sends the class a postcard and a photo.

"He's at a construction zone! I knew it!" kids called out.

"Yes! He's at a real construction site! That's pretty cool! Let's read this postcard together and find out what he's been doing!" I placed the postcard under the document camera. "I'll start . . ."

I placed my finger below the word *Greetings*, and stammered, "*Gr . . . Grrrrr*? Forget it. This is too much work." I pushed the postcard aside and huffed and puffed, crossing my arms.

We know that some of the words children will encounter, such as head *or* great, *won't follow the pattern they might expect of a vowel team. Scanlon, Anderson, and Sweeney (2007) advocate teaching children the strategy of "vowel flexing." If children view vowels as decision points in their reading, they can be prepared to try several different sounds while keeping in mind the meaning of the text. It can help to teach children to work through a little order of operations, first trying the long sound of the first vowel, and then short sound before doing the same with the second vowel. Of course, there are also vowel teams that make a whole new sound, and these will be the focus of upcoming bends. The point is that no one rule will work to solve every word, and therefore being flexible is a critical skill for your readers.*

"Nooo!!" the kids protested.

"Are you saying I should be the boss of my reading?" The class nodded. "You're right. I'd better try something to solve this word. Well, I see a part I know, *Gr* . . ." I slid my finger under the next part, pointing out a familiar vowel team. "Oh! I see a vowel team! Remember, whenever you spot a vowel team in a tough word, it's decision time! "You can ask yourself, 'How am I going to try this vowel? I can look at the first vowel and try the long sound. If that doesn't work, I can try the short-vowel sound. And if that doesn't work, I can try the long and short sound of the second vowel. I can keep trying the word different ways until it makes sense and sounds right.'"

I turned back to the word. "Hmm, . . . I know the first vowel in a vowel team usually makes a long sound, so I'll decide to try a long *E* sound first, /eeeeeeee/. *Gree* . . ." I continued to move across the word, "*Greet* . . . Oh and I know this part, too, *ing, greeting, greetings*! Yes, that's a word I know! *Greetings* is another way to say 'Hello!'" I read the remainder of the sentence:

Greetings from New York City!

"Rasheed is in New York City! Wow! I wonder what he's up to! Let's keep reading. Remember, when we see a vowel team, it's decision time! We'll try it one way, then another to solve the word."

Guide children to read the word *been*, pointing out how not all words and vowel teams work the same way. They should check the words to make sure they make sense and sound right.

I have b—

"A vowel team! *EE* just like in *greetings*. Let's try the long-vowel sound again, /bēn/?" I filled in, making a long *E* sound. "I see that *EE* vowel team, again, but *beeeeeen* with a long *E* doesn't make sense! I think I'll decide to try the short *E* sound next, /bĕn/. 'I have *ben*'? Hmm, . . . I'm not sure that fits. Oh, forget it."

The class protested. "Okay, you're right, I need to . . ." I sang a lyric from our song, "'. . . try something else, and don't give up!'

"Hmm, . . . I could try the second vowel . . . but it's also an *E*! That won't help. I'm going to have to try something else!

"Okay, maybe it would help to take a running start. Let me reread and think what would fit here. 'Greetings from New York City! I have *b—been*? I have been in the Big Apple!' Yes, I think that works! I have *been*, not /bēn/ or /bĕn/.

"Interesting . . . even though this word has *EE*, like in *see*, it doesn't work the same way. It's important to watch out for times when a word doesn't work the way you think it will. It's not enough to just check the letters. You need to make sure your reading always makes sense and sounds right."

We went on to read the next three sentences, stopping to solve words featuring vowel teams the class had been studying, including *nearly*, *street*, *roads*, and *train*. I paused at vowel teams to cue students to help make a decision, trying

---

Notice how you'll offer students an opportunity to discover exceptions to how vowel teams typically work, in context as opposed to working with examples in isolation. This allows readers to monitor and self-correct for meaning.

We recognize that some of these examples may not work, depending on your accent and dialect. Some people do pronounce the word been *with a long E sound, or use /bēn/ and /bĭn/ interchangeably. If that is the case for your students, continue reading and do this same work when you get to the word* learn.

While the vowel team in learn *is r-controlled, you won't want to point this out to kids just yet. You'll offer more explicit practice with r-controlled vowels in the next unit. For now, reinforce the strategy of trying the vowel sound another way, and thinking about what makes sense.*

the sounds more than one way to solve and check the word. When we solved the word *learn*, I pointed out how the vowel team was not making a long sound in this word either.

> *I have been in the Big Apple! There are construction sites on nearly every street.*
>
> *This is the perfect place to learn more about building!*
>
> *Workers are busy building roads and train tracks and skyscrapers.*

RUG TIME

Set up partners to read the rest of Rasheed's postcard, focusing on words with vowel teams they've been studying, *EE*, *EA*, *AI*, *AY*, and *OA*. Coach kids to stop at vowel teams to make a decision about their sounds.

"Will you work with your partner to read the rest of Rasheed's postcard? Remember, bosses, it's important to use everything you know to solve and check your reading. When you come across a vowel team, it's decision time! Try the first vowel two ways. If that doesn't work, try the second vowel two ways. Just remember to always be thinking about what makes sense.

"I'm going to pass out some pens. When you spot any of the vowel teams we've been studying, *EE*, *EA*, *AI*, *AY*, and *OA*, circle them."

I quickly distributed copies. Then, I moved around the rug as partners read the next stretch of text:

> *Yesterday, I read signs that said, "Keep Out!" and "Stay Back!"*
>
> *You need to be really careful when you build.*
>
> *I think that's true when you read, too.*
>
> *I can't wait to see you!*
>
> *Rasheed*

I coached kids to look out for vowel teams to solve words like *yesterday*, *read*, *said*, *keep*, *stay*, *need*, *really*, *wait*, *see*, and *Rasheed*. I listened in to observe how kids pronounced *read* in the past tense in the first sentence. Many tried the long sound and I prompted them to check if it sounded right. Later, I coached students to check the present tense of *read* in the text. "*Read* and *read* look exactly the same," I pointed to each word on the postcard, "but they sound different. You'll need to check that the word you say makes sense and sounds right. If not, you can try it another way."

I also listened carefully as students approached the word *said*, many recognizing it as a snap word. I prompted readers to notice the vowel team *AI* making a different sound to support their ability to approach vowels with flexibility.

POSSIBLE COACHING MOVES

▸ "'If you think something's wrong, you've got to *stop*!' I see a vowel team! Decision time!"

▸ "'Then you try something else, and don't give up!' Try the first vowel sound another way. Doesn't make sense? Try the second vowel."

▸ "'When you think you've got it right, check it out!' Is that a word you know? Does it make sense and sound right?"

Here, the phrase, "Try it two ways," refers to vowel flexibility, trying both the short and long vowel sound when problem-solving new words. This reading strategy is first taught in Building Good Reading Habits *from the Grade 1, Unit 1,* Units of Study for Teaching Reading.

Pay attention to the way your readers problem solve the word build. *While many students will likely solve this word using the meaning of the text, encourage anyone who gets stuck to use the strategy of vowel flexing (trying out the long and short sounds of the first vowel and then the second). Even though you haven't introduced this particular vowel combination, it provides the perfect opportunity to use this strategy.*

As I circulated among the class, I prompted students to move through the reading process by singing a line from our "Be a Reading Boss" song and then giving a tip to support them in this work.

SHARE • Using Interactive Writing to Make a Warning Sign

Channel students to reread Rasheed's postcard together and study a few words with vowel teams. Point out words they need to watch out for, such as *said* and *been*.

I called for the students' attention and we quickly read Rasheed's postcard chorally together. "I see that you circled lots of words with vowel teams! Well done!

"You noticed that sometimes in words with a vowel team, the first vowel makes a long sound like in the word *wait*," I said, pointing to the word. "But you also noticed that not all words with vowel teams work the same way, like in the words *great* or *said*.

"Rasheed was right! Reading might not be *dangerous* work, like construction, but you do need to be really careful. Remember, if you get to a tricky word and see a vowel team—it's decision time! You have to be the boss. You need to stop and try out a bunch of different sounds, checking to make sure your reading makes sense!

"Maybe we should make a sign for our classroom, like the signs in a construction site, to remind us to *watch out* for words that don't work the same way." I clipped a sheet of chart paper to the easel and wrote "WATCH OUT!" in big letters at the top.

"Let's write a reminder that says, 'Sometimes vowel teams do not make a long sound.'" I quickly wrote the first two words, then paused before the word *teams*. "Listen to the vowel you hear in the middle of the word *teams*. *Teeeeeeeeams*. Yes, a long E. There's a vowel team working to make that sound. Do you think EA is making that sound or EE? Let's write it both ways and decide which one looks right." I used a whiteboard to write the word using both vowel teams, *teams* and *teems*, helping students identify which word looked right. "Yes, the word *teams* uses the vowel team EA. Max, come up and write it on our sign."

I pressed on, quickly writing most of the words, only stopping to hand the pen over to students for words with vowel teams, including *said* and *been*. I also paused before writing the word *make* to think aloud about which long-vowel pattern to use, AI or silent E, first writing *maik*, then calling a child up to edit the word. Then, we reread our sign.

"I bet this sign will help you remember to *watch out* for words that don't work the same way when you read. If you find words in your books with vowel teams that don't make a long sound, like *said*, you can write them on a Post-it and stick them to our warning sign!"

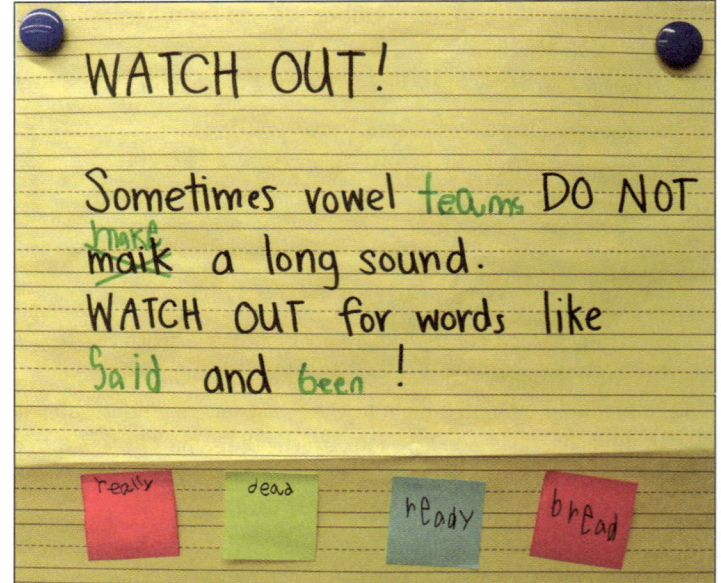

FIG. 5–2 Completed warning sign

EXTENSION 1 • Reading Workshop Word Hunt

Channel students to collect words with vowel teams that make the long-vowel sound and other sounds by looking through their independent reading books and practicing decoding these words.

"Word builders," I voiced over as students looked up from their independent reading books, "you have been hard at work using vowel teams to help you build, read, and write words. I'm sure you've also been noticing them in your books! As you read, keep an eye out for words with vowel teams. Remember, many words have vowel teams that do make the long-vowel sound, like *team* and *keep*—you can keep recording them in your little notebooks. You'll also want to be on the lookout for words with a vowel team that don't make a long-vowel sound, like *said* and *been*. These words can be tricky, but if you remember to try the vowel sounds a few different ways and reread the sentence to think about what's happening in your book, those strategies can help you figure out the word."

"Collect these words in your word builder notebook. Then, later, you can write them on a Post-it note and add them to our warning sign. That way, we can help readers in our school keep an eye out for these kinds of words in their books."

EXTENSION 2 • Add a New Snap Word to the Class Word Wall: *Been*

 GETTING READY
- Display the anchor chart titled "Make it a SNAP word!"
- Be sure children have their whiteboards and markers.

Work with children to go through the steps of "Make it a SNAP word!" to make *been* into a snap word.

"Word builders, if you are going to need to watch out for vowel teams that don't make a long sound in words like *said* and *been*, then it would help to make *been* a snap word, too. That way, you won't be tricked by those vowel teams in tough words in your books. When you know words with vowels that work a different way, it can help you remember to try those vowel sounds a different way until you find the word that makes sense and sounds right!

"Let's study the word *been*. You can spell it, cover, write, check it, and use it so you make sure this is a word you can read and write in a snap. Then, let's add it to our word wall!"

We moved through the steps of the "Make it a SNAP word!" chart. I pointed out that the vowel team *EE* would not make a long *E* sound when you pronounce it as /bĭn/. Then, we chanted its spelling, before the students practiced writing the word on whiteboards. We used the word in several sentences to help anchor its meaning, before adding the word to the class wall.

SESSION 5: WATCHING OUT FOR WORDS THAT DON'T WORK THE SAME WAY

EXTENSION 3 • Transitioning to Partner Time during Reading Workshop

Rally students to continue to pay close attention to signs that they need to stop, slow down, or watch out as they read.

"I've been thinking a lot about what Rasheed told us in his postcard. He made me realize that word builders need to be really careful when they're on the job! Just like there are signs posted around a construction site telling workers to stay back or keep out, there are signs you need to pay attention to when you read.

"When something isn't quite right, it's like a sign pops up in your brain telling you to *stop* and try again.

"Or when you read up to a big, long word, a sign pops up warning you to *slow down* so you don't whiz past the middle or forget to check the ending.

"Or when you see a vowel team and it's not making a long sound, it's another sign telling you to *watch out* for words that don't work the same way. It's important to notice signs that tell you to stop, and to slow down, or to watch out when you read.

"Right now, take turns reading with your partner and remember to pay close attention to any signs telling you to *stop* or *slow down* or *watch out*. Notice when there's a job to be done in your books, then get to work to make your reading even stronger.

"Okay readers, let's go, let's go, it's time to work. Let's go! . . ." I sang out, signalling for partners to get started before moving closer to listen and coach in.

SESSION 6

Word Builders Need Powerful Tools to Get the Job Done

IN THIS SESSION

TODAY YOU'LL teach students that word builders need tools to get the job done. You'll work with children to create a vowel team linking chart to use as a tool as they read and write words.

TODAY YOUR STUDENTS will use their knowledge of vowel teams and vowel patterns and refer to their vowel team linking chart as they read their independent reading books and edit a piece of writing.

GETTING READY

✔ Keep Rasheed hidden away. He is still "away on a trip."

✔ Prepare a blank grid with fifteen boxes on a large piece of chart paper. Use this to create a "Vowel Teams" chart with students.

✔ Distribute whiteboards and markers to each partnership.

✔ Be sure children have their book baggies.

✔ Be ready to display, read aloud, and edit a poem that starts "The rane is falling."

MINILESSON

CONNECTION

Rally children to quickly reflect on everything they've learned about vowel teams and to teach each other.

"Readers, I bet Rasheed will be back any day now! Before he returns, let's make sure we'll be ready to teach him everything we've learned about vowel teams. What are they? How do they work? Do they always work the same way? Turn and teach your partner. Work together to say everything you can about vowel teams!"

I gave the class a minute or so to name back all we had studied across the bend, listening in to assess how well children were able to articulate their understanding of vowel teams. Then, I called the group back together.

"Oh, my goodness! You'll have so much to teach Rasheed when he returns. I heard you say that vowel teams are usually two vowels side by side like *E* and *A* or *A* and *I*, and that the first vowel is usually a long sound, and the second vowel is . . ."

"Silent!"

PHONICS INSTRUCTION

Phonics
- Recognize the spelling-sound correspondence for common long-vowel patterns (*EE*, *EA*, *AI*, *AY*, and *OA*).

Word Knowledge/Solving
- Use knowledge of long-vowel CVVC patterns to decode new words.
- Use knowledge of common long-vowel patterns to edit writing.

High-Frequency Words
- Review and recognize snap words with automaticity.

"I even heard some of you warn your partner to watch out because sometimes the vowel team works a different way, like in the words *said* and *been*."

"And *break* and *head*," voices called out, adding on examples they had discovered in their books.

"Yes! Those words don't have a long sound! Remember, when you see a vowel team in a tough word, it's decision time! You can look at the first vowel and try the long sound because that's the way a lot of vowel teams work, but if that doesn't work, you'll have to try some other ways and think about what makes sense. Wow, word building is a tough job and we need to be really careful!"

❖ **Name the teaching point.**

"Today I want to teach you that builders need tools to get the job done. You can use a chart to remember the sounds vowel teams usually make to help you read and write tough words."

TEACHING

Work with your students to create a linking chart for vowel teams, a powerful tool to help them read and spell new words using parts they know.

"Let's work together to design a special tool to help with those tough jobs, so you can read and spell new words using parts you already know. This is a big job, so we're going to need a big tool." I pulled out a large piece of chart paper, on which I had drawn a blank grid with fifteen boxes, even though I did not plan on filling in every box just yet.

"We can make a chart with the vowel teams we know to remember the sounds they usually make inside a word. Let's see . . . we've studied a bunch of vowel teams so far, like . . ." I tapped my chin, inviting kids to think along with me. Kids began to call out examples, and together we filled in the first five boxes. "Oh! We even have leftover space to make this tool more powerful. Maybe we'll discover other vowel teams to collect here." I quickly moved on.

"Hmm, . . . I don't think this tool is working yet. This can remind us of the vowel teams to look out for but it's not helping remind us of the sounds they make. I know! Let's add a word we know really well. Then, we can use that word to help us read and write new words with the same part."

I tapped on the first box. "*EE* . . . what words do I know really well with this vowel team?" I looked over at the word wall. "Oh yes, we know *see* and *three*. Those are snap words! I also know *tree* and *sheep* and *jeep*! I could add one of those words to this box. I'll pick one . . . *tree*. Let me write it."

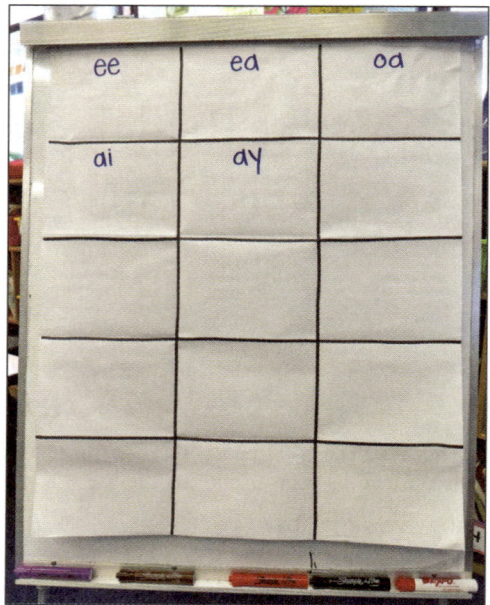

FIG. 6–1 The start of a class linking chart for vowel teams.

If you have taught the additional reading unit, Word Detectives: Strategies for Using High-Frequency Words and for Decoding, *then you may have already introduced a similar linking chart to expose children to the concept of vowel teams and help them decode these words in their books. We recommend starting a new chart, even if some of this may be review for your students. This chart will grow across the unit, starting with vowel teams that make a long-vowel sound in this session and adding diphthongs and other more challenging vowel teams in the next bends. You may choose to change the pictures and linking words in each box to help this feel fresh and new for your students.*

I wrote the word in the first box, underlining the vowel team. "Now our tool is getting charged up. This word can help us remember that *EE* makes the /eeeeeee/ sound like in *treeeeeee*. Oh! I just thought of something. Let's add even more power. Instead of just a word to help remember the sound, let's also draw a picture!" I quickly sketched a picture of a tree above the word. "Thumbs up if you agree that this tool is getting more powerful!" Kids held up their thumbs. "Let's work together to do the same with the other vowel teams we've learned, adding a word we know well and a picture that matches."

We went on to fill in a word and picture for the vowel teams *EA* and *OA*, deciding on *eat* and *boat*.

ACTIVE ENGAGEMENT/LINK

Channel partners to think of *AI* and *AY* words, then write and draw anchor words.

"Help me with the last two boxes on our chart, *AI* and *AY*. Now, you'll have to be careful because both of these vowel teams make the same long *A* sound, /aaaaaaaa/. You'll need to use a word you know that uses the part *AI* and a word that uses *AY*. Remember, you'll usually find *AI* in the middle of a word and *AY* at the very end. You can use the word wall to help you, too.

"I'll hand each partnership a whiteboard. Draw a line to split your board in half and write a word to help you with each vowel team. Then, draw a quick picture." I quickly distributed the materials. Then I observed children as they worked together to write and draw an anchor word. As the rest of the class continued working, I invited one pair to write and illustrate the words *rain* and *tray* on the class chart.

"Will you hold your boards up high, so I can see all of your words? Such great examples . . . *train*, *rain*, *nail*, *wait*, and *play*, *hay*, *spray*, *day* . . ." Together, we reread the anchor words, listening for the long *A* and locating the vowels *AI* in the middle of *rain* and *AY* at the end of *tray*.

Then, we reread the whole chart, saying each anchor word and isolating the long-vowel sound, pointing to the letters in each vowel team.

RUG TIME

Invite partners to read a book, looking for vowel teams. Remind them to use the "Vowel Teams" chart.

"Let's put this tool to use. After all, what's the point of a hammer or a drill or a saw if it just sits in a toolbox and never gets used? You can use this 'Vowel Teams' chart to help you read.

While we have made suggestions as to the words you might use on your linking chart, there is nothing special about these particular words. We encourage you to make any changes that will help this chart to be as engaging and memorable as possible for your students. You might have children with vowel teams in their name, or a toy or game that's all the rage in your classroom. Using these examples will really make this work come to life for kids.

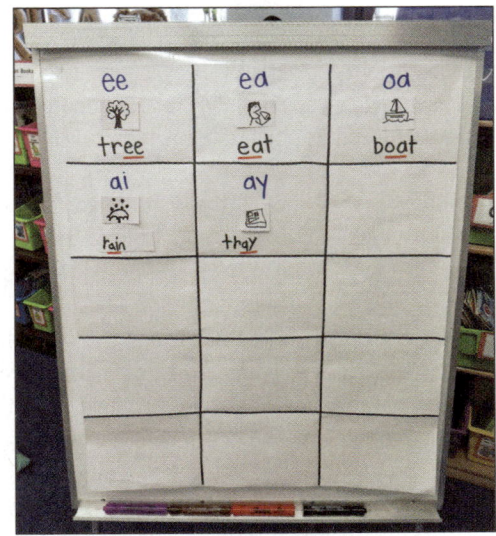

FIG. 6–2 The class adds anchor words and pictures to the "Vowel Teams" chart.

If you haven't already, take a few minutes today to peek ahead and familiarize yourself with the theme song of the unit, which you'll introduce to students at the start of Session 7. You'll also find a copy of the "Word Builder Song" in the online resources.

"Right now, take out your book baggies and choose a book to read with your partner. As you read, you can look out for vowel teams like the ones we've studied. Then, use the tool to check if the vowel is making a long sound, or working in a different way. Ready, readers?" I began to whistle. Then, I sang, "Let's go, let's go."

"It's time to work. Let's go!" kids chimed in. I prompted partners to get started, before moving closer to coach in.

SHARE • Using Vowel Team Knowledge to Write Words and Fix Them

Work with children to use their vowel team knowledge and tool to fix misspelled words in a poem.

I pulled the class back together. "Quick! Put your book baggies away, we have another job to do!" I paused a moment for kids to put their books away, sitting back on top of their baggies. Then, I continued, "Vowel teams are not just important when you read, they're also important when you write! So, writers, let's use our tool to help check and fix up some words in this poem that my little cousin wrote.

"Before we take a look at the words, listen to the poem and picture what's happening." I read the poem to the class. Then we very quickly talked about the images the poem painted, discussing its meaning before moving on to edit the piece.

I placed the poem under the document camera, featuring words with vowel teams that were both correctly and incorrectly used. "Now, as I reread the poem, listen even more carefully for the long-vowel sounds. If you hear a long vowel, give me a stop signal. Then, we can check that the word looks right. If it doesn't, we can use our 'Vowel Teams' chart to try it another way and decide which way looks right."

I read the first line, and children signaled to stop so we could check the word *rane*. "*Rane*? The *rane* is falling. I see a silent *E* at the end, but does this word look right?" I pointed under the word as kids shook their heads, no. "Wait! Check the chart! What vowel team do we need in the word *rain*?" I gestured toward the chart.

"*AI*!" kids called out.

"Wow! Our tool was really helpful that time. *Rain* is the picture we chose for our chart." I wrote *rain* above *rane*, prompting the class to check which word looked right, before crossing out the misspelled word and circling the proper spelling.

We continued through the poem, line by line, stopping at the words *stream*, *street*, *leaves*, *float*, *away*, and *boats*, fixing misspelled words, using our linking chart to find the right vowel team, and confirming words that were spelled correctly.

"We created a pretty powerful tool today—one that helps us read *and* write! I'll keep this chart up so you can use it all day long, during reading workshop and during writing workshop. When you see a vowel team in your books, you can

FIG. 6–3 A student's poem used for interactive editing.

Here you are tucking in a process you'll want writers to make a habit, trying a word more than one way before deciding which word looks right. This work encourages kids to be flexible, especially when spelling with long-vowel patterns.

use the chart to remember the sound that vowel team usually makes, and when you hear a long vowel in a word you want to spell, you can use this chart to help you decide if you need a vowel team to spell it."

EXTENSION 1 • Creating Individualized Linking Charts for Vowel Teams

GETTING READY

- Hand out copies of blank vowel teams chart to partners.
- Children will need their book baggies.

Invite partners to create their own "Vowel Teams" charts to help solve tough words in their own books.

I stood in the middle of reading workshop and called for the class's attention. "Readers, I can tell you are hard at work, solving and checking your words so you can do the most important reading job of all—understand and love your books.

"Remember, the 'Vowel Teams' chart we created during phonics workshop is a helpful tool that you can use during reading workshop! Right now, work with a partner to make your own 'Vowel Teams' tool so you can get the job done when you're working to solve tough words in your books."

I held up a blank grid for students to fill in. Then, pointing to the class chart, I suggested, "First, use our class chart to help you fill in all the vowel teams we've been studying. Then, add a word that uses that vowel team and draw a picture to match! Maybe you'll decide to use the same words we chose together, or maybe you'll use other words you know really well."

I quickly distributed copies of the blank grid for students to use. Then I circulated, coaching in as children chose anchor words for each vowel team, helping them to spell those words accurately on their charts. Once children finished creating their chart, I suggested they keep them in their reading baggies to use whenever they read.

FIG. 6–4 A blank vowel teams chart. Kids will work with this chart again in Sessions 10 and 11.

Having your students begin their linking chart in reading workshop provides a certain level of support as they can use words they see in their books as mentors for their anchor words. You could also invite students to create a linking chart in writing workshop with words they use in their own writing.

You could also consider using this extension with a small group of students. Children learning English will especially benefit from an individualized tool featuring words that are meaningful to them. Generate possible words together on a whiteboard and then help students to add one relevant to them to their charts. You could also use a familiar shared reading text to find well known words together.

EXTENSION 2 • What's My Mystery Word?

 GETTING READY

- Give each partnership ten blank index cards and a copy of the word wall.

Teach students a game in which they give clues to a partner to figure out a mystery snap word.

"Friends, let's play 'What's My Mystery Word?' I'm going to give each partnership a mini word wall and ten blank index cards. Look at the word wall and pick ten words you and your partner want to practice. Then, write one word on each card. Put all the cards facedown so you can't read them. Then, Partner 1, take a card and hold it up to your forehead so you can't see the word—but make sure your partner can see it. Like this." I demonstrated choosing a card from a pile and putting it on my forehead, careful to show I had not peeked.

"Remember, Partner 2, it is your job to help your partner guess the word! You can give three clues. You might give clues about what kind of vowels or vowel teams are in the word, how many syllables or letters there are, what the word rhymes with . . . there are many kinds of clues!

"Let's try! Who can give me a clue about this mystery snap word?" Students raised their hands and I called on one child. "It starts with *W*!"

"Great clue," I said, turning to face the word wall, scanning over the *W* words. "Now I could try to guess. But I think I need another clue." I called on a child who said, "It has a vowel team we learned in the middle." Another said, "It rhymes with *late* . . ." Finally, I guessed the word: *wait*.

Then, I prompted partners to play, while I coached as needed. I reminded partners to take turns.

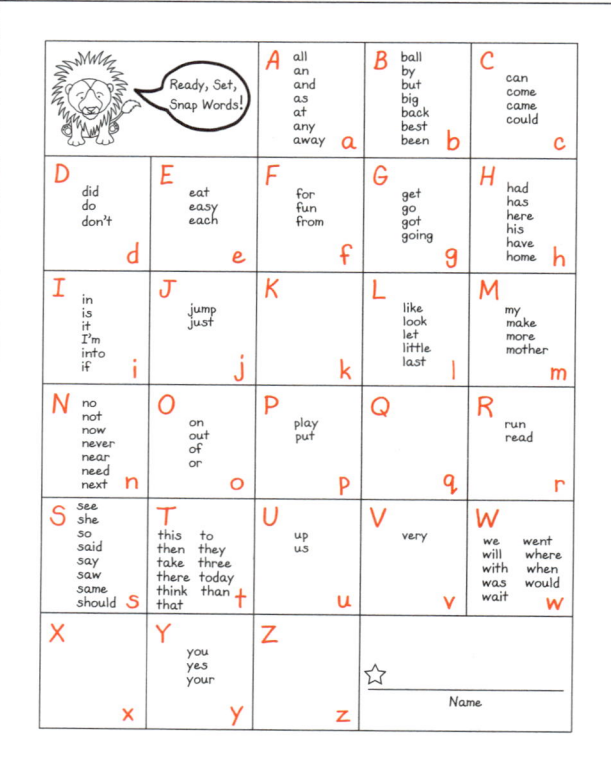

FIG. 6–5 A personal word wall

EXTENSION 3 • A Toolbox Celebration: Tools Help Word Builders Get the Job Done!

Rally partners to gather all their word study tools and teach each other how to use the tools for reading and writing.

"Word builders, you have built quite the collection of tools to help you read and write longer and harder words. Why don't you and your partner take a few moments to gather your tools and pretend your desk is your toolbox? You can celebrate how you've learned to use all the tools in your toolbox! Take out each tool one by one and teach your partner the ways you might use the tool in reading and ways you could use the tool in writing to help you with your words." I watched as kids gathered tools such as their word builder notebook, personal word walls, and the "Vowel Teams" chart. Some students even walked over to the area where the snap cubes were and brought a caddy back to their desk.

As kids shared, I heard them say things like, "When I want to write a word in my writing I can look and see if it's on the word wall or if another word can help me." "I can see if the word in my book has a vowel team." "I can use the chart to help me remember the sound it can make."

End the celebration by reminding children that they have a powerful word-building tool in their own brains.

As the toolbox celebration came to a close, I reminded students of another powerful tool. "Most importantly, you know you have the tools to help you build words in your mind—you have the knowledge of blends, digraphs, endings, vowels, *and* vowel teams. Any time you're reading or writing, you can reach inside your very own brain and think about the parts of words you know to help you read and write longer and more difficult words. Take a bow, word builders!"

BEND II Building Words with Trickier Parts: Studying Vowel Teams that Make Two Sounds

Dear Teachers,

In this bend your students will learn about the vowel teams *OU*, *OW*, and *OO*. Unlike the vowel digraphs you taught in the last bend, your students will not be able to decode words with these letters just by trying the long and short sounds of each vowel. "Some vowel teams are special," you'll tell your students, "because they make a whole new sound."

In Session 7, you'll explain this principle by first examining words with the vowel team *OU* that represents the /ou/ sound, as in *out*. This is a digraph children see frequently in their books, so on this day you'll send kids off to do a word hunt, looking through their independent reading books for *OU* words that also make an /ou/ sound. Then, in Session 8, you'll let kids know that *OU* isn't the only vowel team to make this sound. *OW* can also represent the same sound. This session also acts as a high-frequency word lesson as children take on learning a collection of words with both of these vowel teams.

Your class mascot, Rasheed, will be away visiting construction sites but you will hear from him in a letter he sends back to your class in Session 9. In this letter, he notices that the exact same tool can do two very different jobs. "I wonder if vowel teams work the same way?" he asks. This launches your students into a little inquiry, looking into whether the vowel team *OW* can represent more than one sound. By studying a collection of sentences, students will use meaning along with visual information to decode words with *OW* and think about the sound represented by the vowel team. They'll discover that *OW* can make an /ou/ sound as in *flower*, but also an /ō/ sound, as in *rainbow*. Then at the end of this same session, you'll pull out your shared reading text *Tumbleweed Stew* and repeat the same investigation with words containing *OU*. This vowel team, your students will learn, can actually make a whole bunch of different sounds.

Then in Session 10, children continue to build on this learning by finding out that *OO* is another vowel team that can represent two sounds such as /o͝o/ in *book*, and /o͞o/ in *moon*. To help keep all this information organized, you'll lean heavily on your "Vowel Teams" linking chart, recruiting your students' help in adding to it each day. You'll want to keep this chart prominently displayed over the course of the unit and review it by reading it together whenever you have an extra minute or two.

This bend adds six new snap words to the word wall. The first four (*house, about, down,* and *our*) are learned in Session 8. You students will then add *know* in an extension to Session 9 after learning about the multiple sounds of the vowel team *OW*, and *school* in an extension to Session 10 after learning about the sounds represented by *OO*. After teaching these words, you'll want to add them to your word wall and channel children to continue to practice them throughout the week. You'll notice deliberate attempts to return to these words in extensions, showing children how they can use these words to support them in reading and writing other new words. "*Out* is such a helpful word," you'll say. "If you know *out*, then you can also read and write words like *shout* and *about*." In this way, snap words act not just as an anchor for the vowel team being learned, but also as a reminder of common phonograms children use in their reading and writing.

The bend culminates in Session 11 with Rasheed returning from his travels, eager to hear everything your class has learned about vowel teams while he's been away. This final session acts as a consolidation of learning and a mini-celebration. Students will practice building words with all three vowel teams learned in this bend on their whiteboards and then edit their independent writing, looking out for words that may include any of the vowel teams learned across the first two bends.

All the best,
Havilah, Elizabeth, and Jennifer

SESSION 7

Vowel Teams Can Make *New* Sounds

Learning the Vowel Team OU

IN THIS SESSION

TODAY YOU'LL teach students that some vowel teams work in special ways. You will introduce *OU* in a familiar snap word, *out*. Then you'll demonstrate how *OU* works in the middle of words like *proud* and work with students to add an *OU* word to the linking chart.

TODAY YOUR STUDENTS will break apart words with *OU* in the middle and put them back together again to figure out what they say. They will also hunt for *OU* words in their books and write them down.

MINILESSON

CONNECTION

Invite children to sing a song about word building. Then rally them to learn a new vowel team.

"Let's go, let's go. It's time to work. Let's go!" I sang as the children settled on the rug. "Do you remember this song I keep singing? I wrote some words to fit the work we are doing as word builders. Will you sing it with me before we go off to work today?" I clipped the lyrics to the easel and began singing. (See Fig. 7–1 on pae 48.)

"Wow! You sound like you are ready to get right to work and that's a good thing because you've got an extra big job to do today! You already know a bunch of vowel teams such as *EA*, *EE*, *AI*, *AY*, and *OA* that we can find in words," I said, gesturing to our new vowel team chart. But did you know that there are even more vowel teams? And some of these vowel teams are extra special."

❖ **Name the teaching point.**

"Today I want to teach you that some vowel teams work in special ways. Instead of a long-vowel sound, vowel teams like *OU* work together to make a new sound. *OU* usually makes the sound /ou/."

> ### GETTING READY
>
> ✓ Display lyrics to the "Word Builder Song."
>
> ✓ Be ready to draw Elkonin boxes on the easel and have highlighter tape on hand.
>
> ✓ Prepare to display word cards for *sour*, *count*, *loud*, *mouse*, and *ground*.
>
> ✓ Ask students to bring their book baggies to the carpet.
>
> ✓ Distribute Post-it notes to students.
>
> ✓ Display and add to the class "Vowel Teams" linking chart from Session 6.

PHONICS INSTRUCTION

Phonological Awareness
- Isolate and pronounce initial, medial vowel, and ending sounds in spoken single-syllable words.
- Change the beginning, ending, or middle phoneme to make a new word.

Phonics
- Hear and identify the vowel sound in words, locating the letters that represent the sound.
- Recognize and use letter combinations that represent unique vowel sounds to decode words with a CVVC pattern (*OU*).
- Recognize and use phonograms with a unique vowel sound to build and read new words (-*oud*, -*ound*, -*ouch*).

Word Knowledge/Solving
- Use knowledge of phonograms as well as digraphs, blends, and inflected endings to build words.

TEACHING

Introduce the vowel team *OU* in a familiar snap word, *out*. Explain how *OU* usually makes the /ou/ sound and doesn't make a long-vowel sound like some other vowel teams.

"Let me show you what I mean." I held up the word *out*. "I took this word right off our word wall. You already know this word in a snap. It says . . ."

"*Out*!" the class called out.

"Yes! At the start of this word you can see this new vowel team, *O* and *U* side by side. Let's double-check the sound it's making." I quickly drew two Elkonin boxes on the easel.

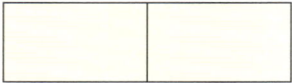

"Will you say the word *out* slowly as I push the sounds into each box?" As the class stretched the word *out*, I moved my index finger into the box that corresponded with each sound. "I'm hearing two sounds, /ou/ and /t/." I wrote the letters into the boxes.

"This vowel team isn't making a long-vowel sound like some other vowel teams we know. Instead, it's making a whole *new* sound that you'll have to remember. *OU* usually makes the sound /ou/. We can use our snap word *out* to remind us of this sound." I took a piece of highlighter tape and highlighted the vowel team to be used as a reference on the word wall.

"I have another way to help us remember the new sound this vowel team makes," I said with a smile. "James, will you come up here and pinch me?" James looked at me incredulously and then gave my arm a gentle pinch. "Ow!!" I exclaimed. "Oh!" I said, pointing to the letter *O* in the vowel team. "You . . ." I pointed to the letter *U*, ". . . pinched me!"

The class giggled. "If you ever forget the sound this vowel team makes, just remember the time James pinched me and I said 'Ow!! Oh, you pinched me!'"

Demonstrate how the *OU* vowel team might work when it's in the middle of a word, *proud*.

"Now let's use what we know about the sound *OU* usually makes to read a word that has this vowel team hiding in the *middle* of the word." I quickly wrote the word *proud* on the board. Running my finger under the word, I demonstrated the way I would break up the word.

FIG. 7–1 Lyrics to the unit's theme song

"This first part is a blend we know, /pr/. Then I see the vowel team *OU*, which makes the sound /ou/, *pr . . . ou*. And at the end I see a *D. Pr . . . ou . . . d, proud*! I was very proud of how hard I worked today!" I added, providing some context for the word.

I quickly wrote the letters *OU* on the easel, under the word *proud*. "Say /ou/ when I point to this vowel team," I said, pointing under the letters *OU*. "Now let's read this word again." I ran my finger under the word *proud* as the class read the word together.

proud

ou

ACTIVE ENGAGEMENT/LINK

Recruit children to break apart words with *OU* in the middle and put them back together to figure out what they say.

"Now it's your turn to try reading some more words with the vowel team *OU* hiding in the middle. Will you work with your partner to do some demolition? Break these words apart and put them back together to figure out what they say." I displayed a series of five word cards on the easel, all containing the vowel team *OU*.

I listened in as students worked to decode these words, prompting them to say the sound of the vowel team in isolation and then read the whole word. I then brought the class together to read and check the list of words.

You may want to have some whiteboards on hand if students have a hard time decoding these words by looking at them on an easel. Sometimes the act of writing a word down can help children attend more closely to all the parts.

RUG TIME

Channel children to hunt for *OU* words in their books and write them on Post-its.

"This is going to be such a helpful vowel team because I know that there are words with *OU* all through your books. Will you take out your reading baggies and take a look? Read through your books and go on a hunt for words with vowel teams. Pay especially close attention for words with *OU*. If you find one, you can jot it on a Post-it. I'll pass some out as you start reading. Let's go, let's go!" I began singing.

"It's time to work. Let's go!" the class called back as they opened up their books. As students began reading, I circulated among the group, coaching as needed.

POSSIBLE COACHING MOVES

- "Look carefully at all the parts of the word, especially the middle!"
- "That word has the vowel team *AI*. Remember, it usually makes a long *A* sound. Try that!"
- "You found a word with *OU*. Remember what sound it usually makes? Use the word *out* to help you."
- "Does that make sense? If not, try the sound another way. Remember, vowel teams don't always work the same way."

SHARE • Adding an *OU* Word and Picture to the "Vowel Teams" Chart

Ask children to think of *OU* words that might be added to the linking chart. Then choose one example and invite kids to draw and write the *OU* word with a magic pen.

"We've learned a new vowel team today, so let's add it to our 'Vowel Teams' chart. That way we can use this tool to help us remember *all* the things we know about vowel teams as we read and write." I wrote the vowel team *OU* in the next box on the linking chart.

"Let's think. What word would be helpful to remind us of the sound *OU* usually makes? Think of the words you found in your book today! Turn and talk to your partner." I listened in as students talked, mindful of the fact that not all the words suggested would necessarily be spelled with the *OU* vowel team. I then brought the class together.

"I heard some great ideas! I heard *house*, *out*, *mouse*, *cloud*, *shout*, and *mouth*. Those would all be great words for our chart. I'm going to pick *cloud* to add to our tool. Can you take out your magic notebooks," I said, holding up one of my hands like a pretend notebook, "and a magic pen?" I held out the index finger on my other hand as if it was a pen. "First draw a picture, then write the word *cloud*. Say it slowly to help you." As students worked I invited one child up to help me write the word on our chart, filling in the vowel team in the middle of the word, and drawing a quick illustration.

We encourage you to swap the suggested word and picture in each box of this linking chart for an example that is relevant and interesting to your students. This is a great place to make use of children's names.

If you chose to also have children make individual linking charts as described in Session 6, Extension 1, you may want students to take those out of their book baggies right now and add their own word to their linking charts. Perhaps you could have them pick a word to write and illustrate from the selection you brainstorm together.

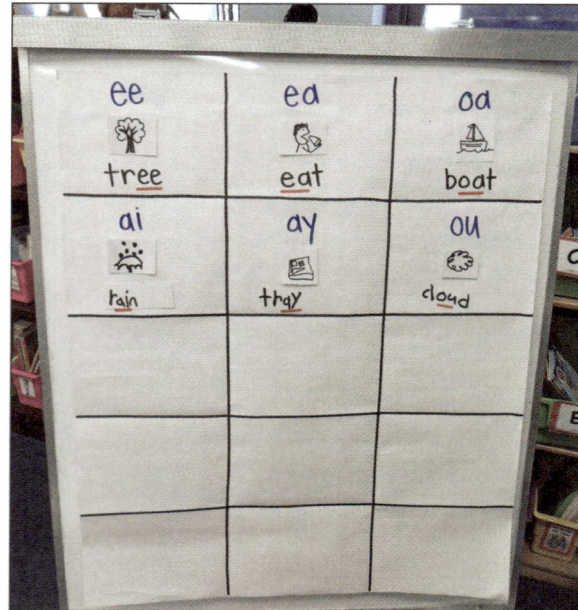

FIG. 7–2 The class adds *cloud* to anchor the sound of *OU*.

EXTENSION 1 • Building Words with *OU* Phonograms

GETTING READY

- Be sure students have whiteboards and markers.
- Prepare word cards for *proud*, *loud*, *louder*, *clouds*, *found*, *sounds*, *around*, and *ground*; *couch*, *pouch*, *grouch*, and *crouching*.

Invite children to build *OU* words by noticing word patterns and using word parts such as digraphs, blends, and endings.

"Word builders! Does everyone have their materials ready?" I scanned the group, checking to see that everyone had a whiteboard and marker. "Ready to do some construction? Let's start with a word you already figured out today—*proud*. I was *proud* of how hard I worked," I said, putting the word into context. "Say it slowly to help you figure it out."

As children wrote the word *proud* on their whiteboards, I placed the card in the pocket chart. "Check that you've spelled it right!" I called out. "We want to be a careful work crew!

"Now change some letters and see if you can turn *proud* into *loud*. The music was very *loud*." I once again added the word card it to the pocket chart. "Now add the letters *ER* to the end of that word. What does this say now? Turn and tell your partner. See if you can figure it out. Now take the word *louder* and turn it into *clouds*. I saw puffy *clouds* in the sky."

In this way, we continued building words. I alternated between telling students the word, asking them to spell it and telling them what letters to use, asking them to read it. Each time, I provided the word in a sentence and added it to our pocket chart. We went on to make the words *found*, *sounds*, *around*, and *ground*; *couch*, *pouch*, *grouch*, and *crouching*.

If you plan on completing the next extension, you'll want to avoid putting the words in neat columns organized by phonograms. Place them randomly in your pocket chart so that you can come back to these words later and search for common patterns.

EXTENSION 2 • Sort Words from Session 7, Extension 1, into Common Phonograms

Channel students to listen closely to notice word endings and identify similar patterns. Then re-sort the words on your pocket chart based on phonogram patterns such as *-ouch*, *-oud*, and *-ound*.

"As you worked earlier to build new words, I couldn't help but admire the way you used parts you know to help you spell. You not only used the vowel team *OU* but also digraphs, blends, and endings. Let's reread the words again together. As we read, make sure also to listen closely to the end of each word." As we read through the words placed randomly in the pocket chart, I emphasized the sound at the end of each word.

"I wonder if you're noticing any other ways we could group these words." I paused a moment, giving children a chance to study the words on the pocket chart. "Do you notice any patterns that are the same?" Kids began pointing out words with common phonograms, like *pouch*, *grouch*, *couch*, and *crouching*.

As children called out their observations, I began to re-sort the word cards into new columns.

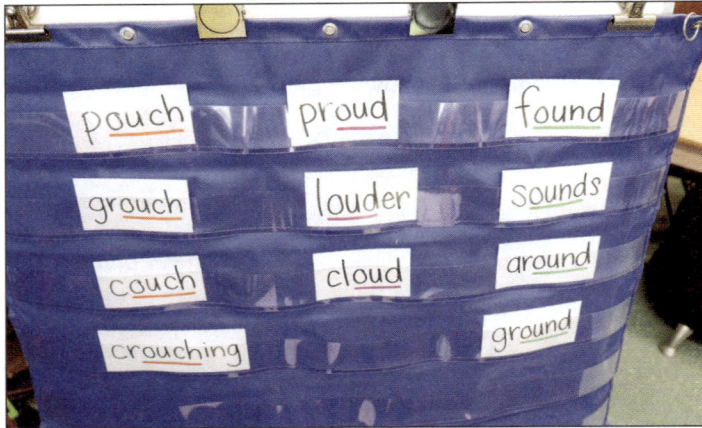

"These patterns can be a big help when you read and write! When you see a pattern like *-ouch*, *-oud*, or *-ound* . . ." I quickly underlined the phonogram in each word, ". . . you can think, 'Do I know a word that ends the same way?' When you know a word like *found* it can help you read and write words like *grounded*, *pounding*, or *surround*!"

If children need more support finding these phonograms, you'll want to provide more explicit direction. You might pull a word like couch *from the pocket chart and ask children to locate another word that ends with the same pattern and also sounds the same.*

SESSION 8

Using *OU* and *OW* to Learn New Snap Words

IN THIS SESSION

TODAY YOU'LL teach students there are two ways to make the /ou/ sound in a word, *OU* and *OW*. You'll invite kids to read a story along with you, looking for *OU* and *OW* words, studying them, spelling them, and turning them into snap words.

TODAY YOUR STUDENTS will use *OU* and *OW* to figure out words, study them, spell them, and turn them into snap words. Expect them to decode words by identifying vowel teams in the middle of words and sort words by vowel teams.

MINILESSON

CONNECTION

Show how *OU* isn't the only vowel team that makes the /ou/ sound.

"Word builders, I was writing an email this morning and just as I was about to type the word *now*, I thought 'Oh! That word has an /ou/ sound! Just like *ouuut*!'" I said, pointing to the word wall. "And just like *clouuud*!" I said, pointing to our linking chart. "So, I used our new vowel team to write that word and spelled it like this." I held up a word card with the letters *NOU* written on it.

"That's not how you spell it!" a few voices called out.

"You're right!" I laughed. "As soon as I saw it, I knew it didn't look right!" I put the word card down. "So, then I checked the word wall, and there it was!" I stood up, walked over to the word wall, and took the word down. Pointing under each letter I spelled the word. "N-O-W . . . now."

"How interesting! It looks like *OU* isn't the only way to make the /ou/ sound in a word! You can also use the letters *OW* to make an /ou/ sound." I put some highlighter tape across the *O* and *W* in the word *now* and placed it on the easel.

GETTING READY

- Print the story "My New Home" and have a highlighter or highlighter tape ready.
- Be sure each student has a whiteboard and dry erase marker.
- Display your "Make it a SNAP word!" anchor chart and "Vowel Teams" linking chart.
- Make a word card for the word *nou* (misspelling of *now*).
- Prepare word wall cards for *house*, *about*, *down*, and *our*.
- Prepare a set of the same word cards for each rug club.
- Be ready to sing the "Word Builder Song" from the previous session.
- Prepare a set of word cards for *town*, *clown*, *frown*, *sound*, *found*. Be ready to sort them in a pocket chart.

PHONICS INSTRUCTION

Phonological Awareness
- Change the beginning, ending, or middle phoneme to make a new word.

Phonics
- Distinguish between two vowel patterns that make the same sound: *OW* and *OU*.

- Recognize and use phonograms with a unique vowel sound to build and read new words (-*out*, -*own*).

Word Knowledge/Solving
- Use knowledge of vowel patterns and digraphs, blends, and inflected endings to build words.

High-Frequency Words
- Learn four new words: *house*, *about*, *down*, *our*.

✤ Name the teaching point.

"Today I want to teach you that there are two ways to make the /ou/ sound in a word, *OU* and *OW*. You can use these parts to read and write lots of new words. You can even use these parts to help you turn new words into snap words!"

TEACHING AND ACTIVE ENGAGEMENT/LINK

Invite students to read a story along with you, looking for words with *OU* or *OW*, studying those words, and spelling them.

"I have four new snap words for you to learn today—words that you will see a lot in your reading and use a lot in your writing. And just like the words *out* and *now*, these words are built with an *OU* or *OW* vowel team. To learn these words, I thought we'd do something a little different today. I found a story that has all four of these words in it. Let's read this story together and stop when we notice a word with *OU* or *OW* to study it closely."

I placed the story "My New Home" under the document camera and invited students to read along with me, articulating just the first sound in the word *house* before stopping.

My New Home

We are moving to a new h____ (house).

"Hmm, . . . what word would make sense here?" I asked, pausing to let students shout out what they were thinking.

"*Home*!" called some voices. "*House*!" others chimed in. "Let's take a closer look. What do we notice in this word?"

"*OU*!" the class shouted.

"Right! Okay, remember, when you see a vowel team, it's decision time! We know *OU* usually says /ou/. Let's try that sound first and check if it works." I ran my finger under the word as we all said *houuuuse*, stretching the word out slowly. I then reread the sentence.

"That looks right and makes sense! You just found and read our first new snap word! Will you now take a little time to study it?" I placed some highlighter tape over the word in the story and placed the snap word card under the document camera, so we could study the word in isolation. "Turn and tell your partner everything you notice about this word." I gave students just a brief moment to talk, before naming out some of the things I heard.

"I heard people say this word has five letters. It has an *OU* vowel team that makes the sound /ou/, just like *out* and *cloud*. And some of you noticed a silent *E* at the end, but this silent *E* doesn't seem to be changing the vowel sound. Interesting.

Your students might be confused when you refer to OW as a vowel team. After all, W isn't a vowel. If this comes up, let them know that a vowel team can be two vowels, but it can also be two letters that work together to make a vowel sound. In this case the W acts like a vowel because it works together with the O to make one vowel sound.

FIG. 8–1 A story that includes new snap words.

"Now, let's spell it!" Together, we chanted the letters before going back to the text. "Let's keep reading and see if we can find another word with *OU* or *OW*. If you see one, give me a stop signal," I held up my hand, "so we can study it."

I continued reading the story, stopping at the words *about*, *down*, and *our*. Each time, I highlighted the word in the story. Then, we studied the word in isolation, and spelled it by chanting the letters. After pausing to learn each new snap word, I reread from the start of the text to help students maintain meaning.

RUG TIME CLUBS

Set children up to write the snap words they just learned.

"Did you realize that while we were reading the story, we were also going through our steps to turn a word into snap word?" I pointed to our "Make it a SNAP word!" anchor chart. "We read our words, studied them, and spelled them! Now it's time to get to work writing them. This is a super-important step because writing words down really helps them to stick in our brain."

You'll notice that we move through these familiar steps to learn new snap words in a different way across this lesson, incorporating an opportunity for children to acquire new high-frequency words by first studying them in the context of a story.

"I'm going to give each rug club a stack of snap word cards. Put them facedown in the middle of your group. One person draws a card. Read the word to your group and *use it* in a sentence." I pointed to the last step on the chart. "You can show everyone the word, so they can take a picture in their brain, and then cover it up! Everybody else in the rug club

You'll want to make sure your new snap words get added to your word wall after today's session.

SESSION 8: USING *OU* AND *OW* TO LEARN NEW SNAP WORDS

55

can write it down. Don't just write it once, fill up your whole board. If anyone needs help, ask the person holding the card. Then erase your boards and the next person in the group can draw a card.

"Let's sing our 'Word Builder Song' together as we make a circle with our rug clubs and get our cards ready. Let's go, let's go." I began singing as I passed each group a stack of word cards, and soon the room was filled with a chorus of voices getting ready to work.

As students began practicing their snap words, I circulated among the group, prompting in as needed.

> **POSSIBLE COACHING MOVES**
>
> ▶ "Read that word to your whole group. Remember that the *OW* vowel team makes an /ou/ sound."
>
> ▶ "Write it again! Can you write it even faster? Remember, fast doesn't mean sloppy. Make sure you can still read all the letters in that word."
>
> ▶ "Check that word! Do a slow check and see if you have all the parts you need. D—owww—nn. Yes! You have all the parts of that word."

SHARE • Reading and Learning More Words with *OU* and *OW*

Rally children to use the *OU* and *OW* vowel teams to review snap words and learn new words.

"Knowing that *OU* and *OW* can *both* make the /ou/ sound in a word is going to be so helpful when you're reading! Let's practice reading some words with those vowel teams. I have a stack of words here. Some of these are words you know well . . . maybe even in a snap!" I said with a smile. "And some of these are new words."

I held up the word card *down* and the class shouted it out enthusiastically. "Yes! Now you know that word in a snap!" I placed the word in a pocket chart, starting a column for words with *OW*. Then I held up the word *house*. We read it together and placed it in the pocket chart at the top of a second column for words with the letters *OU*.

"Here are the rest of the words," I said, displaying five more words on the easel. Will you read them with your partner? Then, we'll check them together."

I listened in as students worked to decode these words, prompting them to notice the vowel team in the middle of the word. I then brought the class together to check each word, identify the vowel team, and place it in the appropriate column in the pocket chart.

"Wow! Word builders, you sure know how to use vowel teams to help you solve new words quickly. You used the vowel teams *OW* and *OU* to read those words in a snap!"

EXTENSION 1 • Adding Word Endings to Build New Words

GETTING READY

- Prepare a stack of cards with common endings, including *-ing*, *-ed*, *-s*, *-er*, and *-es*. Also prepare word cards with some words that your children have been studying, such as *rain*, *frown*, *teach*, *feel*, *clean*, *float*, *paint*, *loud*, *need*, *reach*, and *grow*.
- Be ready to give each partnership one baggie of endings and one baggie of words.
- Be ready to demonstrate making new words with the cards.

Channel children to make new words by using words they know and adding endings, keeping in mind that not all endings make real words.

"You have been working so hard to learn about vowel teams that I am a little worried you may have forgotten about other word parts, like endings. Have you?" I asked, smiling. "No!" the class replied.

"Let's remember the different word endings you see when you read and use when you write. Then, you'll use those endings to play a game with your partner." I gathered a stack of cards with common endings written on each, including *-ing*, *-ed*, *-s*, *-er*, and *-es*. Kids read each ending aloud, as I held up each card.

"Fantastic! Remember, endings can help us change what a word means and how we use it in a sentence.

"I have two baggies for each partnership. One baggie has a set of endings and the other baggie has some of the words we have been studying together. You can build new words together with your partner by combining a word with an ending." I held up the word *rain* and the ending *-ing* and put them together to make *raining*. "I've heard this word before. And I can use it in a sentence, 'I should get my umbrella because it's raining outside.'

"The catch is, not all endings will make real words." I continued to hold the word *rain* but picked up the ending *-er* and pushed them together. "*Rainer*?" I said with a puzzled look on my face. "I haven't heard that word, and I don't think I could use it in a sentence.

"As you work to build a new word with these endings, you can give that new word a little test by reading it together, thinking, 'Have we heard that word before?' Then, if the word works, invent a sentence together. It's time to work . . . let's go" I distributed baggies to partnerships.

FIG. 8–2 Adding endings to words with vowel teams.

EXTENSION 2 • Using Snap Words to Build New Words with *OU* and *OW*

 GETTING READY

- Be sure children have their word builder notebooks (same notebooks children used in Session 6, Extension 3).
- Be ready to take the words *out* and *down* off the word wall and take them to the meeting area.

Explain to students that they can continue to study vowel teams *OU* and *OW* by creating phonogram charts in their notebooks. They can use word wall words such as *out* and *down* to get started.

"Word builders are always on the lookout for new building projects. They take their notebooks with them wherever they go and jot down the words and word parts they want to remember. You can find ideas for new building projects by starting with the words you already know well," I pointed to the class word wall. "You can use snap words to build brand new words!

"Right now, let's take two snap words off the word wall to do some building. Grab your word builder notebooks and meet me in the meeting area."

After children had assembled, I said, "Let's start with the word *out*." I displayed the word wall word. "This word *out* can be so useful. You can add a letter or two to the beginning to get so many new words. Watch me use *out* to get some new ideas for words. I'm going to use this chart paper as my notebook to record some new ideas I have for words." I wrote *out* at the top of a piece of chart paper and then said, "If I add *sh* to the beginning of *out* I can get the word . . ." I let my voice trail off as kids chimed in with the word *shout*. I wrote *shout* underneath the word *out* and underlined the part -*out* in *shout* to emphasize the phonogram. "That's right, if I add the digraph *sh* to *out* I get *shout*.

"Work with your partner to add to the list. Think about letters or blends or digraphs you can add to the beginning of *out* to help you build new words. Record those words in your notebook." I noticed kids trying out words such as *snout*, *pout*, *spout*, and *about*.

We then repeated the same process with the snap word *down*.

As partners work you might coach in, reminding students to try new words out loud by substituting different parts at the beginning of the words before jotting them down. Inevitably, some students will write down nonsense words and you can prompt them to check if all their words are ones they've heard before.

SESSION 9

Investigating the Sounds of *OW* and *OU*

IN THIS SESSION

TODAY YOU'LL guide students in an inquiry to see how the vowel team *OW* does different jobs in different words. You'll work with them to study sentences with *OW* words and figure out if the vowel team sounds like /ou/ in *flower* or like /ō/ in *know*. You will add *OW* words and pictures to the "Vowel Teams" linking chart.

TODAY YOUR STUDENTS will study *OW* words to answer the inquiry question, "Can the vowel team *OW* do different jobs and make more than one sound?"

MINILESSON

CONNECTION

Read aloud a letter from Rasheed and show his two photos of exactly the same screwdriver. Point out that one tool can do two different jobs.

"I'm so excited! We got a letter from Rasheed and I can't wait to read it! It feels like he's been gone for so *long*! Aren't you wondering how he's doing?" I took the letter out of an envelope, placed it under the document camera, and began reading.

"Good news! Rasheed is coming home soon! I bet you can't wait to see him." I looked back at the letter and tapped the word *tools*. "But what's he talking about here? What tools?" I peered into the envelope and pulled out a second sheet of paper. "Wait! There's something else in here. Maybe this will help."

I placed the sheet under the document camera, revealing two photographs of the exact same screwdriver. "Huh?" I scratched my head. "These don't look like two different tools! They look exactly the same! Oh, look! There are captions under the pictures. Let's read them."

GETTING READY

✓ Print the letter from Rasheed and place it in an envelope.

✓ Prepare a collection of sentence strips with *OU* and *OW* words to sort in a pocket chart.

✓ Prepare copies of sentence strips with *OW* words and put them in baggies, one set for each rug club.

✓ Display and add to your "Vowel Teams" linking chart.

✓ Have *Tumbleweed Stew* by Susan Crummel on hand to display pages 5 and 6 under the document camera. Mark the words *house*, *about*, *through* with highlighter tape.

PHONICS INSTRUCTION

Phonics
- Distinguish between the two sounds one vowel pattern makes for the vowel pattern *OW*.
- Hear and identify the vowel sound in words, locating the letters that represent the sound.
- Recognize and use letter combinations that represent unique vowel sounds to decode words with a CVVC pattern.
- Distinguish between the many sounds one vowel pattern makes for the vowel pattern *OU*.

High-Frequency Words
- Learn one new high-frequency word: *know*.

I pointed to the captions and read, "Cabinet Attacher," and "Doorknob Installer." "Interesting!" I said. "Rasheed seems to be telling us that the exact same tool can do two totally different jobs. Now I'm *also* wondering if vowel teams work the same way. Can one vowel team do two totally different jobs? Let's study the vowel team *OW*. We already know it makes the sound /ou/. I wonder if it has another job. Let's work together to answer this question."

♣ **Name the inquiry question.**

"Can the vowel team *OW* do different jobs and make more than one sound?"

TEACHING

Guide students to study sentences with *OW* words and to figure out how some *OW* words sound similar, while others do not.

"I have a bunch of sentences that have a word with *OW*. Let's read these sentences, figure out what the *OW* word is and then study the sound the vowel team makes. If it makes the /ou/ sound like *now*, then we'll put the word on this side of our pocket chart," I said, pointing to the left side of our chart. "And if it makes a different sound, we'll put it on the other side."

I revealed the first sentence strip and began reading it, stopping at the word *flower*.

I gave my mom a flower.

"Here's a word with *OW*! Let's do some demolition and break this word up to figure it out. Placing my finger under the blend at the start of the word, I said, "This first part says . . . /fl/. Are you thinking what would make sense in this word? 'I gave my mom a fl . . .'"

"*Flower!*" some voices called out.

"Let's do a slow check to see if you're right." I ran my finger under the word, saying it slowly to demonstrate checking all the parts. "Yes! This word says *flower*. That makes sense and it looks right. Will you listen to the sound the *OW* team is making?" I read the word once more, emphasizing the vowel team in the middle. "It sounds like this word is making an /ou/ sound, just like the word *now*." I underlined the word *flower* and then placed the sentence strip on the left side of the pocket chart.

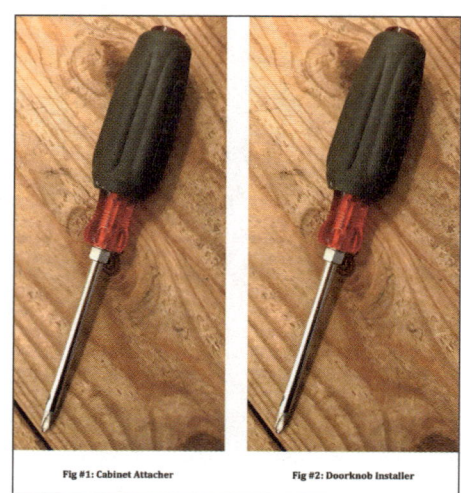

FIG. 9–1 A letter from Rasheed suggesting one vowel team can make more than one sound.

You'll notice we have children do this work in the context of a sentence. It is critical that they be able to cross-check for meaning to confirm whether they have the correct pronunciation of a word. For example, mispronouncing the word know *as* now *still makes a meaningful word. But when students hear that pronunciation in the context of a sentence, they'll be cued to self-correct it.*

I then revealed a second sentence.

> Do you know what time it is?

I began reading this time stopping at the word *know*. "Aha! Another word with *OW*. I underlined the word. Let's figure this one out." I placed my finger under the *KN* at the start of the word. "I know that a *K* and *N* together make the sound /n/. Let's think what would make sense. 'Do you kn . . .'"

"*Know!*" the class called out again.

"*Do you know what time it is?*" I read. "That makes sense! Let's investigate what sound the *OW* is making this time." I read the word *know* once more, again emphasizing the vowel team. "Hmm, . . . say that word slowly to yourself and tell your partner what sound you think *OW* is making. Does it sound like /ou/ in *now* and *flower*, or is it making a new sound?"

I gave students just a few seconds to talk and then brought them together. "I heard people say that this word sounds different! It sounds like *OW* is making an /ō/ sound. How cool! This one vowel team is doing two different jobs and making two different sounds!" I took the sentence strip and placed it on the other side of the pocket chart.

FIG. 9–2   Sorting sentences with the sounds of *OW*.

ACTIVE ENGAGEMENT/LINK

Channel partners to find *OW* words in sentences and figure out how the words sound, like /ou/ in *flower* or /ō/ in *know*.

"Here's another sentence," I said, holding up a third sentence strip. This time will you read this one with your partner and see if you can decide which side of the chart it should go on? Find the word with *OW*, read it and ask, 'Does it sound like /ou/ in *flower*, or does it sound like /ō/ in *know*?'"

> After the rain, we saw a rainbow.

I circulated among the group, listening in to the ways partners were problem solving this sentence. "Look for the word with the *OW*," I prompted. "Say it slowly. Listen to the sound *OW* makes. Where should I put it on my pocket chart?

"You found out this word says *rainbow*!" I said, pulling the class together. "And most of you decided that in this word the *OW* is making an /ō/ sound, just like the word *know*." I read the sentence, underlining the word *rainbow*, and placed it in the right-hand side of the pocket chart.

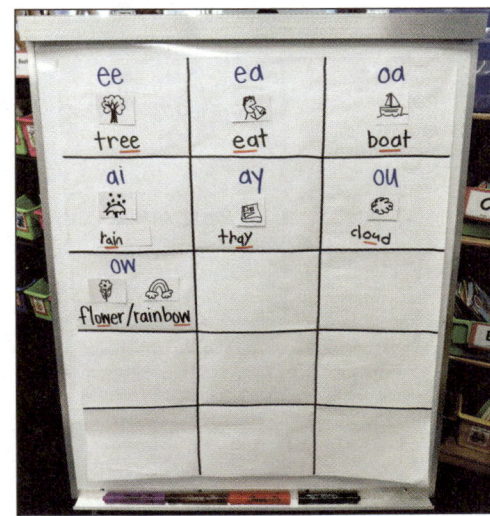

SESSION 9: INVESTIGATING THE SOUNDS OF *OW* AND *OU*

"Rasheed was right! There are vowel teams that do more than one job and make more than one sound. Now whenever you see a word with *OW* in your books, you'll know it's decision time! You can decide which sound to try first, /ou/ or /ō/, trying it one way, and then the other way to figure out which way makes sense.

"I'm going to add the words *flower* and *rainbow* to our 'Vowel Teams' chart to help us remember the two sounds of *OW*." I quickly drew the two pictures on the chart.

RUG TIME

Invite rug clubs to read sentences with words with *OW* and figure out how to say those words, trying both /ou/ or /ō/ sounds and thinking about what makes sense.

"I'm going to give each rug club a baggie of cut-up sentences just like the ones we put in the pocket chart. Each of these sentences has one or two words with *OW*. Work together to read these sentences. To help you figure out the words with *OW*, remember to try both sounds, /ou/ and /ō/, and think about what makes sense.

"Let's go, let's go. It's time to work. Let's go!" I sang, handing each group a baggie of sentences. Then I moved among the class, listening in and prompting as needed.

> Wow! Show me how fast you can run now.
>
> Look how big you are! You have grown up so much!
>
> Some dogs growl if they are afraid.
>
> "Hoot! Hoot!" said the little brown owl.

POSSIBLE COACHING MOVES

- "Check the chart. Try it one way, then try the other way if you need to."
- "Does that make sense? Take a running start. What would make sense that starts with ____?"
- "That word has *OW*. Is it making a sound like *flower* or a sound like *rainbow*?"
- "Is there another word with *OW* in this sentence?"

SHARE • Digging into the Tricky *OU* Vowel Team

Work with students to figure out the different sounds *OU* can make in different words.

"Now that we know *OW* can make *two* different sounds and do *two* different jobs, that's got me wondering about the vowel team *OU*. We already know that *OU* can make an /ou/ sound in a word, like *out* or *cloud*. But does it make any other sounds? Let's do a little investigation."

I opened our familiar shared reading text from reading workshop, *Tumbleweed Stew*, to pages 5 and 6 and placed the two-page spread under the document camera. "You already know this book well from our shared reading. On these two pages there are a whole bunch of words with *OU* and I've highlighted them for you. Will you work together with your partner to read these words? Then check them! Is the *OU* making an /ou/ sound like *out* or does it make a different sound?"

I gave students a few moments to work with their partners and then brought the group together to name some of the things I'd heard. "It sounds like a lot of you were saying that *OU* is making different sounds, not just the /ou/ sound we already know. Thumbs up if you agree.

"Some of you noticed the sound *OU* makes in the snap word *would*." I isolated the vowel sound, making an /o͝o/ sound like the *OO* in *look*. "Some of you noticed that it can make an /o͞o/ sound like in the word *you*," I said, pointing to the word in *Tumbleweed Stew*. "And some of you noticed that it can also make an /ô/ sound, like in the word *thought*!" I pointed to the highlighted word under the document camera.

"It seems like *OU* is a vowel team that actually makes a lot of different sounds. This makes it extra tricky when we want to figure out a new word in our books. Remember, you are the boss. You need to decide how you'll help yourself solve a word when you see *OU*. You can try the /ou/ sound first. Most of the time, this will work. If it doesn't, think, 'What would make sense?' Then try out a few different sounds to see what fits."

Tumbleweed Stew is the shared reading text that accompanies the unit Readers Have Big Jobs to Do: Fluency, Phonics, and Comprehension, *from the first-grade Units of Study for Teaching Reading. We're assuming your students have already read this text multiple times with your support. If not, you'll want to swap out the text in today's share for another familiar book, displaying a page that contains some words showcasing the multiple sounds of* OU.

The vowel team OU can represent a number of different sounds such as /ou/ in house, */ō/ in* dough, */o͞o/ in* soup, */ô/ in* bought, *and /ŭ/ in* trouble. *Children can be easily confused if they're expected to remember all of these different sounds. As they develop more sight words, they will begin to differentiate between these sounds by recognizing common phonograms such as -ough or -ound. For the time being, it's sufficient to let them know that the most common variation is the /ou/ sound they have already learned, but also make it clear that they will need to be flexible when problem solving these words.*

EXTENSION 1 • Turning *Know* into a Snap Word

 GETTING READY

- Make sure students have whiteboards and markers
- Display the "Make it a SNAP word!" anchor chart.
- Be ready to add the snap word *know* to the word wall.

Work with children to apply the steps of "Make it a SNAP word!" to make *know* into a snap word.

"Word builders, the vowel team *OW* can be a little tricky. We learned that *OW* can make the sound /ou/ like in *how*, and the sound /ō/ like in *know*. If you are going to need to watch out for vowel teams like *OW* that make two sounds, it can help to make *know* into a snap word to help you remember one of those sounds.

"Let's study the word *know*. You can spell it, cover, write, check it, and use it so you make sure this is a word you can read and write in a snap. Then, let's add it to our word wall!"

We moved through the steps of the "Make it a SNAP word!" chart. I pointed out the first two letters in the word *know* and told kids that *KN* at the beginning of a word makes the sound /n/. Then we studied the vowel team *OW* and noticed it came at the end of the word. We chanted its spelling, and then the students practiced writing the word on whiteboards. Finally, we used the word in several sentences to help anchor its meaning, before adding the word to the class wall.

EXTENSION 2 • Reminding Readers to Watch Out for Vowel Teams *OU* and *OW* in Reading Workshop

During reading workshop, remind students to watch for words with *OU* and *OW* vowel teams and to decide what sounds they might try as they figure out the words.

From the middle of the room during reading workshop, I voiced over, "Reading bosses, I hope you're remembering what you've been learning to solve tough words with vowel teams like *OW*. Remember, during phonics workshop, we learned that *O* and *W* team up to make two sounds, /ou/ and /ō/. And *OU* usually makes /ou/ but sometimes it makes a different sound, like in the words *soup* or *tough*.

"As you read, look out for these parts, and when you see a vowel, decide what sound you'll try first to get the job done. Check if that word makes sense and sounds right. If not, try it another way. And remember, our 'Vowel Teams' chart can help you remember the sounds those parts usually make." I gestured to the class linking chart.

"If you're stuck, stick a Post-it on that page so you can work on it with your partner." I signaled for the class to return to their independent reading work, before moving in to confer with students.

SESSION 10

The Two Sounds of OO

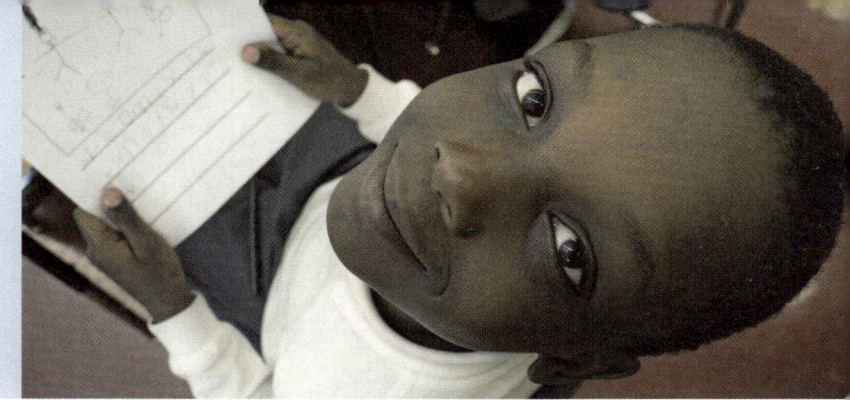

IN THIS SESSION

TODAY YOU'LL teach students to distinguish between the two different *OO* sounds, /o͞o/ like *moon* and /o͝o/ like *book*. You will guide them to play a game of listening to *OO* words and to identify which word does not belong in a group. In the share, you will challenge children to sort *OO* words by noticing phonograms.

TODAY YOUR STUDENTS will learn to identify the two different sounds of *OO*, partners will sort words based on their sounds, and notice common phonograms.

MINILESSON

CONNECTION

Invite children to play a game to listen closely to words, especially the middle. Say the words *school*, *room*, *book*, and *moon* and challenge kids to identify which word sounds different in the middle.

As students gathered in the meeting area, I pulled out a stack of word cards but kept them facedown so kids couldn't peek. Then I smiled and leaned in, whispering to the kids. "I have a little game for us to play. Are you up for a challenge?"

"Yes!" kids replied.

"To play this game, you will need to listen closely to the words I say and tell me which word doesn't belong. And I'll give you a little tip—listening to the *middle* of the word will help you play the game." I gave the class a way to signal me during the game. "You can give me a thumbs up if you have an idea." Then I started in with a little song:

GETTING READY

✓ Prepare a set of sixteen word cards for yourself and for each rug club: *school*, *food*, *spoon*, *broom*, *loop*, *scoop*, *pool*, *room*, *moon*, *stool*, *good*, *wood*, *stood*, *hook*, *cook*, and *book*. Prepare a baggie with these word cards for each rug club.

✓ Be ready to put *OO* word cards in your pocket chart, with one column for words that sound like *moon* /o͞o/ and the other for words that sound like *book* /o͝o/.

✓ Display and prepare to add *OO* words and pictures to your "Vowel Teams" linking chart.

PHONICS INSTRUCTION

Phonological Awareness
- Isolate and hear different medial vowel sounds in spoken single-syllable words.

Phonics
- Distinguish between the two sounds one vowel pattern makes for the vowel pattern *OO*.
- Hear and identify the vowel sound in words, locating the letters that represent the sound.
- Recognize and use letter combinations that represent unique vowel sounds to decode words with a CVVC pattern.
- Recognize and use phonograms with a unique vowel sound to read and build new words (*-oop, -ool, -oom, -oon, -ood, -ook*).

High-Frequency Words
- Learn one new word: *school*.

> One of these sounds is not like the others,
> one of these sounds just doesn't belong,
> can you tell which sound is not like the others . . .

I let my voice trail off as I held up the first card facing toward me, making sure kids were ready to listen but not yet look at the word.

"School," I said slowly before moving on to the rest of the words. "Room, book, moon."

Several kids smiled and signaled with a thumbs up that they had heard the change in the vowel sound when I read the word *book*.

"I see some of you heard the word that's not like the others. The middle of the word *book* doesn't sound like the middle of the words *school*, *room*, and *moon*. Thumbs up if you agree!"

I placed the word cards on the easel. "But, guess what! *Book* may sound different than *school*, *room*, and *moon*, but the vowels are the same!" I pointed to the vowel team in the middle of each word.

❖ Name the teaching point.

"Today I want to teach you that the vowel team *OO* makes *two* new sounds, /o͞o/ like *moon* and /o͝o/ like *book*."

TEACHING

Guide children to study the *OO* words *book* and *moon* and to distinguish the different sounds for *OO*.

"Let's take a closer look at these words." Pointing to the word *book*, I said, "I see the vowel team *OO* in this word." I quickly wrote the letters *OO* under the word *book*. "In this word, I hear the sound /o͝o/. Say /o͝o/," I reminded kids, pointing under the letters *OO*. "Now let's read this word again." I ran my finger under the word *book* as the class read the word together.

> book
>
> oo

"Now what about this word, *moon*?" I pointed to the next word card. "I see the same vowel team, *OO*, but in this word I hear /o͞o/. Say /o͞o/." The class echoed back with the sound, as I wrote the vowel team under the word *moon*.

> moon
>
> oo

If students have a hard time discerning between the two sounds of OO, invite them to say the set of words along with you, paying attention to how the sound of each word feels in their mouth.

"Now read the word with me." Together, we read *moon*, as I pointed under the vowel team in the middle of the word. "*OO* is another vowel team that works in a special way! It makes two new sounds. Sometimes it can sound like /o͞o/ as in *moon* and other times it can sound like /o͝o/ as in *book*."

ACTIVE ENGAGEMENT

Play another round of the *OO* word game, channeling partners to listen closely and signal each other when they hear a word that doesn't belong in a group of *OO* words. Sort these words on your pocket chart.

"Let's test this out by playing another round of our game. This time, could you and your partner listen closely and give each other a signal when you think you know the word that doesn't belong?" The class nodded and moved closer to their partners to get ready for the second round.

FIG. 10–1 Sorting the two sounds of *OO*.

I picked up a set of three words and then started in with the song:

   One of these sounds is not like the others,
   one of these sounds just doesn't belong,
   can you tell which sound is not like the others . . .

I filled in with the words *wood*, *hook*, and *pool*. Several partners signaled each other with a thumbs up when they heard the word *pool*.

"You heard it again, word builders," I congratulated the class. Then I turned to the pocket chart I had hung on the easel, placing the word *moon* on the left side and the word *book* on the right, making two columns.

"You know that the vowel team *OO* can make two sounds, /o͞o/ like in *moon*," I pointed to the word cards in the pocket chart, "and the sound /o͝o/ like in *book*." I pointed to each column, accordingly. "*Wood* and *hook* sound like . . ."

"*Book*!" kids filled in. I placed the words in the right column.

"And *pool* makes /o͞o/ like in . . ."

"*Moon*!" the children called out as I placed the card in the pocket chart.

SESSION 10: THE TWO SOUNDS OF *OO*

RUG TIME CLUBS

Rally children to be the boss of their own learning. Channel clubs to study each word, listening for the *OO* vowel sound in the middle, then sorting word cards into two piles for words that sound like *moon* and *book*.

"You know what I just realized? You don't need *me* to teach you every word there is. When it comes to reading, you are the boss! You can use what you already know about *OO* to read lots of words, trying both sounds to check which words make sense and sound right.

"So, I have a job for you. I have a baggie of words for every rug club. Work together to read each word, listening for the vowel sound in the middle, /oo/ or /oo/. You can make two piles just like we did with these words." I pointed to the pocket chart on the easel. "Words like *moon* can go in one pile and words like *book* can go in another.

"As you start working, I'm going to add a picture of a *book* and a *moon* to our vowel team chart to help us remember the two sounds of *OO*. Off to work you go!"

I distributed one baggie of sixteen word cards to each rug club.

As students began working, I quickly drew the two new pictures on the linking chart and then circulated among the group, coaching as needed.

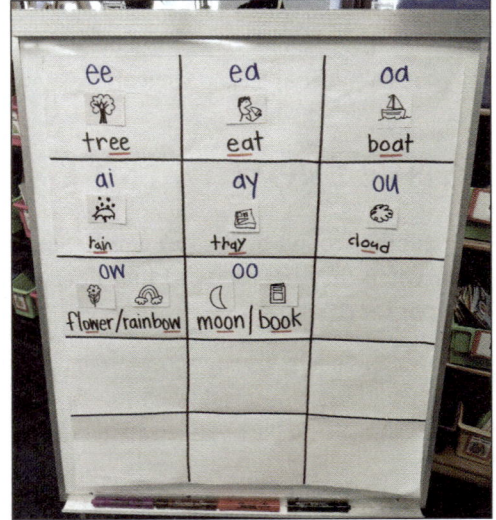

FIG. 10–2 Adding *book* and *moon* to the "Vowel Teams" chart.

> ### POSSIBLE COACHING MOVES
>
> ▸ "Say the word slowly and listen for the vowel. Does it sound like /oo/ in *school* or /oo/ in *good*? Remember, *OO* makes both of those sounds."
>
> ▸ "Is that a real word? Does it make sense and sound right?"
>
> ▸ "After you read each word, give it a s-l-o-w check to make sure it looks right."
>
> ▸ "Read through each pile of words. Does *OO* make the same sound in those words?"
>
> ▸ "Mix them up and sort them again. This time, get the job done even faster!"

SHARE • Recognizing Common Phonograms in OO Words

Channel students to review words sorted by *OO* sounds.

Once every group had sorted through their collection of words at least once, I quickly sorted my set of words in the pocket chart. Then, I called the group back together.

"As you worked I couldn't help but admire the way you looked carefully across each word from start to end, using the sounds *OO* makes to figure it out. You piled up words with /o͞o/ like *moon* and words with /o͝o/ like *book*. I added those words to the pocket chart. Let's read down each list and listen for the vowel sounds." As we read down each column, I emphasized the sound in the middle of each word.

Challenge students to sort *OO* words in a different way, asking them to notice phonogram patterns and checking to see if the words look the same and sound the same.

"I wonder if you're noticing any other ways we could group these words." I paused a moment, giving children a chance to study the words on the pocket chart. "Do you notice any patterns that are the same? Check to see if they look the same and sound the same." Kids began pointing out words with common phonograms, like *spoon* and *moon*, and *hook*, *cook*, and *book*.

As children called out these observations, I began to re-sort the word cards into new columns.

"Patterns like *-oon*, *-ool*, *-oop*, *-oom*, *-ood*, and *-ook*, can help you read and write so many words." I quickly underlined the phonogram in each word. "You can think, 'Do I know a word that ends the same way? Or do I know a word that sounds the same?' When you know a word like *spoon*, it can help you read and write words like *noon*, *cartoon*, or *balloon*!"

We recognize that some of the words such as broom and room could go in either column depending on your accent and punctuation. You will want to make the necessary adjustments based on your context.

If children need more support finding these phonograms, you'll want to provide more explicit direction. You might pull a word like spoon from the pocket chart and ask children to locate another word that ends with the same pattern. Then ask them to read both words and check that they both sound the same. For example, good and food look the same, but they do not sound the same, so they would not get grouped together in the pocket chart.

FIG. 10–3 A completed sort for the two sounds of *OO*.

FIG. 10–4 Sorting words with the OO vowel team by phonogram.

EXTENSION 1 • Making the Word *School* into a Snap Word

GETTING READY

- Display and refer to your "Vowel Teams" linking chart.
- Display the "Make it a SNAP word!" anchor chart.

Work with children to move through the steps of "Make it a SNAP word!" to make *school* into a snap word.

"Word builders, I was studying the linking chart and noticed the word *school* under the vowel team *OO* could help me spell so many other words. If I know *school*, I can spell *pool* or *tool* or even *drool*." We all laughed about the last word.

"It would help to make *school* a snap word, too. That way, if you don't have your linking chart handy you can still look up at the word wall when you need to write a word that sounds like *school*. Also, the word *school* can remind you about the vowel team *OO*—that *OO* can make two sounds.

"Let's study the word *school*. You can spell it, cover, write, check it, and use it so you make sure this is a word you can read and write in a snap. Then, let's add it to our word wall!"

We moved through the steps of the "Make it a SNAP word!" chart. I pointed out that the word *school* started with a three-letter blend and that the vowel team makes the /oo/ sound. Then, we chanted its spelling, before the students practiced writing the word on whiteboards. We used the word in several sentences to help anchor its meaning, before adding the word to the class wall.

EXTENSION 2 • Generating More Words to Add to the List of OO Phonograms

GETTING READY

- Display your pocket chart of *OO* words from the share.
- Provide Post-its to partners.

Remind children that when they make more *OO* words using phonogram patterns, they should make sure the new words sound the same and look the same.

"Word builders, you found lots of different word patterns with the vowel team *OO*, like *O-O-K* in the words *book* and *look*, or *O-O-L* in *pool* and *school*. Paying attention to these patterns can be so helpful because you can use them to build so many other words. Will you get together with your partner, and try this right now?

Repeated practice with phonics principles is critical for students. You can use this extension and others in this book at any time to help support kids as they learn about vowel teams.

"First, pick one pattern from the words we sorted in our pocket chart. Then see if you can think of some more words that you could add to that list. Work with your partner to write them down on a Post-it. Then, grab another Post-it and try another pattern!

"But be careful! You need to make sure that the words you try out sound the same and also look the same. For example, if I was thinking of a word that sounds like *good*," I said, pointing to the word in the pocket chart, "I might pick the word *could*. Say them both with me."

"*Good . . . could*," we said together.

"Do they sound the same? Yep. Now let's check if they look the same. You know the word *could*. It's a snap word!" I quickly wrote the word on the easel. "Does it also look the same? No! So, I won't add that word to our list in the pocket chart. This is tricky work. If you're not sure if you're spelling a word right, try it out on your Post-it and ask, 'Does that look right?' If you're still not sure, put a question mark beside it and we can check it together later.

"Get started! If you want a little tip, try the pattern *O-O-K* first. I bet you can find a lot of words to add to that list! After some work time, you'll have a chance to come up and stick your Post-its on our pocket chart. Let's go, let's go!" I sang out, "It's time to work. Let's go!"

EXTENSION 3 • Updating Individualized "Vowel Teams" Linking Charts

GETTING READY
- Display class "Vowel Teams" linking chart.
- Make sure children have their own "Vowel Teams" charts from Session 6, Extension 1.

Invite partners to add to their personal "Vowel Teams" charts to help solve tough words in their own books.

During reading workshop, I signaled for the class's attention. "Readers, we have learned a lot of new vowel teams over the last few days. You'll want to make sure you have your 'Vowel Teams' chart updated with all the parts you know."

"Take out your chart and fill it up like a toolbox, with all the new parts you can use to solve words." Then, pointing to the class linking chart, I suggested, "Check our class chart to help you fill in the vowel teams we've studied recently. Then, add a word that uses that vowel team and draw a picture to match! Remember, you can always use the same words we chose together, or another word you know really well."

I circulated, coaching in as children added an anchor word and illustration for each vowel team. I reminded children that they might need two words to represent two sounds. As children finished updating their charts and got back to work reading, I encouraged them to use this tool whenever they needed it, to solve words in their books.

If you haven't already encouraged students to make their own linking charts, now is a great time to do so. If you notice some students have difficulty finding words or spelling them correctly, as they add to this tool, you can pull them into a small group for more support. You may turn to familiar texts from shared reading or shared writing to locate anchor words.

SESSION 11

Reviewing Vowel Teams to Build New Words
OU, OW, OO

GETTING READY

✓ Position Rasheed in the meeting area beside three photographs of New York City.

✓ Display your "Vowel Teams" linking chart.

✓ Prepare copies of a page of pictures including illustrations of *moon, spoon, books, cooking, mouth, loud, flower, snow*. Distribute one copy per partnership.

✓ Make sure students have whiteboards and markers, writing folders, and editing pens.

PHONICS INSTRUCTION

Phonological Awareness
- Isolate and pronounce initial, medial vowel, and ending sounds in spoken single-syllable words.

Phonics
- Consolidate learning by writing CVVC words with the vowel teams *OU, OW,* and *OO*, as well as digraphs, blends, and endings.
- Use knowledge of long and unique vowel CVVC patterns to edit words.

High-Frequency Words
- Review and recognize snap words with automaticity.

IN THIS SESSION

TODAY YOU'LL remind students that there isn't just one way vowel teams work, so they'll need to try vowels in different ways when they read and write. You'll elicit what they know about special vowel teams *OO, OU,* and *OW*. You'll also remind them to use tools like the "Vowel Teams" chart and the word wall to help them read and write words.

TODAY YOUR STUDENTS will share what they've learned about special vowel teams *OO, OU,* and *OW*. Expect them to use tools like the "Vowel Teams" chart and the word wall to help them read and write words. They will also use their knowledge to inspect their own writing, listening to and looking for vowels in their words.

MINILESSON

CONNECTION

Examine Rasheed's photos and discover that builders create different buildings in different ways. Connect this to the idea that vowels work in different ways, too.

"Everyone, come quickly! Rasheed just got back, and he wants to share some photos from his trip!" I ushered the class to the meeting area. I propped the class mascot on a nearby shelf surrounded by photographs.

Once the students had settled in their rug spots, I began. "Rasheed, welcome home! Are these photos you took on your trip?" I scooped up three photographs.

Then, sifting through them, I remarked, "Wow! New York City is filled with so many different kinds of buildings—tall ones and short ones . . ." I held up a photograph of the skyline. "And round ones," I held up another photo, this time showing the Guggenheim. "Oh! Look at this one shaped like a triangle!" I held up a photograph of the Flatiron Building.

Word Builders: Using Vowel Teams to Build Big Words

"And those buildings are made in so many different ways—some with glass, others with brick or stone or steel! I think Rasheed brought us these photos to teach us something about building." I turned to the lion. "Is that right, Rasheed? Yes, he wants to tell us that builders create different buildings in different ways—and he wants to remind you that vowels work in different ways, too."

❖ **Name the teaching point.**

"Today I want to remind you that there isn't just one way vowel teams work. Word builders need to use everything they know, trying vowels more than one way, when they read and when they write."

TEACHING

Invite children to teach Rasheed everything they've learned about vowel teams—and at the same time, informally assess their growing understanding.

"Word builders, if you are going to be able to use vowel teams to read and write, it's important to remember the different ways those vowel teams work. Now that Rasheed has returned, let's teach him everything we've discovered about vowel teams." I gestured toward the class linking chart. "We can teach him about vowel teams that make a long sound like *OA*, and other vowel teams that work together to make a new sound, like *OU*." I invited the class to name out some things they had learned about vowel teams.

"The first vowel makes a long sound and the second vowel is silent," Harper began.

"Can you give an example?" I nudged.

"Like in *eat* and *boat*," she added, pulling words from the "Vowel Teams" chart.

"Now is that always true? Do these vowel teams *always* make a long sound?" I prodded.

"Noooooo! Watch out for *said*," voices called out, pointing at our interactive writing warning sign, "and *been*!"

ACTIVE ENGAGEMENT/LINK

Elicit from children what they know about special vowel teams *OO*, *OU*, and *OW*. Remind them to use tools like the "Vowel Teams" chart and the word wall to help them read and write words with these vowel teams.

"Are there vowel teams that work in a special way?" The class began to call out the vowel teams we had studied. "Yes! Vowel teams like *OO*, *OU*, and *OW* make new sounds," I said, pointing to the class linking chart.

FIG. 11–1 Rasheed visits famous buildings in New York City.

Today's lesson is designed to review and reinforce students' growing understanding of vowel teams. You'll want to use this as an opportunity to assess what students are able to articulate about vowel teams. Use these observations to plan for small groups that offer students repeated practice.

SESSION 11: REVIEWING VOWEL TEAMS TO BUILD NEW WORDS

"Quick, turn and tell your partner what you know about these special vowel teams. What sounds do they make? Give some examples. Rasheed will listen in." I prompted partners to talk and I walked around, holding the class mascot, so we could both listen in.

Then, I called the group back together. "Rasheed is very impressed. He thinks these new kinds of vowel teams are pretty tricky. He said you need to be really careful that you don't use the wrong letters when you are writing words or the wrong sounds when you are reading. He's right! Good thing we have a tool that can help us when the job gets really tough!" I gestured toward the "Vowel Teams" chart.

"And that's not the only tool! Remember, our word wall can help! You can use snap words that have these special vowel teams, like *out* and *school* and *now* and *know* to help you with these letters and sounds."

You'll notice that we use the term "vowel team" as an umbrella term to describe all the letter combinations that work together to make a vowel sound. Some of these vowel teams are diphthongs. This term refers to the sound the vowel team makes. A diphthong starts as one vowel sound and moves toward another. You should feel your jaw moving as you articulate these sounds. Examples of diphthongs include OU and OW, covered in this bend, and OI and OY coming up in the next bend.

RUG TIME

Channel partners to identify each picture, and listen to the sounds that they hear across the whole word, especially the vowel team in the middle. Then ask kids to write down each word and do a slow check.

"Let's do some word building to show off what we know about vowel teams! I have some work orders for each pair of word builders." I held up a sheet of pictures. "Look at each picture, say the word, and listen for the sounds you hear. You'll want to listen closely for the vowel team in the middle. You can use our 'Vowel Teams' chart to think about which vowels are working together to make that sound. Then, write the word on your whiteboards and check if it looks right. If not, try it another way!

"Rasheed will be the official building inspector, so make sure to build each word with the right parts. Get to work, word builders!" I prompted partners to take out their whiteboards and markers. Then, I quickly distributed a page of pictures featuring vowel teams we had studied. I carried the class lion with me as I listened in to coach students, helping children to isolate the vowel sound and use the linking chart to identify the team that makes that sound. When students weren't sure, I suggested they try spelling the word more than one way and choose the vowel team that looked right.

As you observe students at work, pay special attention to the way they spell words with OU and OW. If you see writers confusing these vowel teams, prompt them to try it both ways, looking for the word that looks right. Of course, children will not always know what looks right and you'll want to support them in making this decision. You might also prompt them by asking, "Do you know another word that sounds the same? If you know look, *then you can figure out* cooking."

SHARE • Word Builders Can Be Their Own Word Inspectors

Encourage students to be their own word inspectors, inspecting their own writing and listening to and looking for vowels in their words.

"Word builders, eyes up here! Rasheed says you've all passed inspection. You listened carefully to the sounds you heard from the beginning to the end of each word, especially the vowel sound in the middle. Then, you used parts you know to build those words, doing a slow check to make sure the whole word looked right. Job well done!

"Here's the thing—you can be your *own* word inspector. You can inspect your own writing, listening to and looking for vowels in your words. You can use our class 'Vowel Teams' chart to check and fix up words that don't look right. Then, you can give your writing a stamp of approval!"

I prompted students to take out their writing folders and inspect their words. As children worked to edit their pieces, I voiced over, reminding them to listen for long vowels as they reread their writing, stopping to check if those words looked right.

You might consider widening the range of this activity by channeling various groups of writers to check for the phonics features that require continued reinforcement, such as word endings, blends and digraphs, or snap words.

EXTENSION 1 • Reviewing Snap Words as the Word Wall Grows

GETTING READY
- Display the "Make it a SNAP word!" anchor chart.
- Be sure students have their whiteboards and markers.

Invite partners to practice trickier or newer snap words to help "cement" them in their minds.

I fastened the "Make it a SNAP word!" chart to the easel and then stood before the word wall as partners gathered with their whiteboards and markers. "Just like buildings grow up and up as the construction crew adds more and more floors, our word wall is growing, too. I noticed we have added several new words alongside some of our old ones.

"Before the word wall gets any bigger," I widened my arms to emphasize the expanding nature of this tool, "it could be helpful to cement some of the trickier or newer words in our minds and make them stick. One way you can do this is to practice with your partner.

"Right now, take a look across the word wall." I scanned the wall with my eyes. "Choose two words you want to practice. Maybe you choose an old word that you use a lot in your writing but have trouble spelling or maybe a new word that is a little tricky. Give me a thumbs up when you have your two words.

"Tell your partner the two words you chose. Together make a little set of four words to practice. Use the 'SNAP word' chart and your dry erase board as you practice. It might help to look closely at all the parts of the word and write each word a few times. Those steps can help you 'cement' the words in your mind!"

EXTENSION 2 • Vowel Team Match-Up

GETTING READY

- Choose twenty word cards from across the unit and be ready to display them so students can play the word game.
- Ask students to bring their own copy of the "Vowel Teams" chart to the meeting area, or print a blank chart for each partnership to quickly fill in.

Rally children to play a game to remember the vowel teams and sounds they've learned so far in the unit.

"Let's play a game to help us remember all the vowel teams and sounds we have learned so far. Meet me at the rug with your copy of the 'Vowel Teams' chart." As kids gathered at the rug, I readied a stack of twenty cards with words from across the unit.

"I'm going to say a word. You'll repeat the word to your partner. When you repeat it, try and stretch the word out and listen for the vowel sound in the middle or at the end. Once you hear the vowel sound look at your chart and think, 'Which vowel team makes that sound?' Then point to the vowel team you think you'll see in that word. Once I see most of you pointing to a vowel team, I'll reveal the word. You and your partner can do a slow check across the word to see if you agree.

"Let's hold a practice round. The first word is *house*. Say the word and remember to stretch it, listening for the vowel sound." I prompted as partners worked together to hear the sound /ou/. Many partnerships pointed to the box containing *OU* on their charts, while some pointed to the box containing *OW*.

"It's time to give the word a slow check. Remember to look closely at the vowel team," I prompted, as I placed the word *house* under the document camera, so it would be large enough for partnerships to check together.

We continued playing the game with the remainder of the cards.

If your students have not been keeping an individualized linking chart, you'll want to print them a blank chart from the online resources to play this game. Before starting this activity, have children record a vowel team in each box, perhaps drawing a quick sketch for just the sounds they have trouble remembering.

Provisioning Our Toolboxes with Vowel Teams that Make the Same Sound

BEND III

Dear Teachers,

This third bend invites students to learn another host of vowel teams, this time, those you can rely on to produce a single new vowel sound, such as /oi/ in *OI* and *OY*. In three separate sessions, you'll challenge children to study two vowel teams side by side, pairing teams that produce the same sound, including *OI/OY*, *EW/UE*, and *AW/AU*.

You'll lean on your class mascot to launch this final bend, discovering that while there are big plans in the works, students are simply not ready to take on such an enormous project—they need more parts to build words. Then, turning to your growing linking chart, you'll discover that there are quite a few vowel teams left to learn. "I wonder if we can learn, not just one, but *two* vowel teams today?" you'll propose, rallying the class to join you for this final stretch. Of course, there are even more letter combinations that produce a vowel sound that you won't teach explicitly—*IE*, *UI*, and *EI*, to name a few. The truth is, less is more. You'll find that it is more effective to help students continue to approach vowels and vowel teams with flexibility, drawing on known words and parts to problem solve unknown words.

In Session 14, you'll help children consolidate their learning, cautioning them to listen closely to help distinguish between different vowel sounds, such as /ou/ (*OU/OW*) and /ô/ (*AU*), as well as to look carefully across words to check that words look right, so as not to confuse one team for another.

Before the unit ends, you'll also introduce the pattern *IGH* that readers will often encounter in their books, teaching them that these letters work as a team to produce the long *I* sound in words like *might* and *high*, two new snap words you'll add to your word wall this week. You'll also teach the high-frequency words *because* and *few*, linking each word to a vowel team you'll study across the bend. You may want to highlight these featured parts before adding the word cards to the class wall, helping students use snap words as anchors for phonics as they work to read and write new words. On the first day of this bend, you'll also teach *much*, *such*, *two*, and *who*, words commonly found in texts at the levels first-graders are apt to be reading. This set of words doesn't feature vowel teams, of course, but you'll want to study their parts just the same, reminding children to approach new words with a constant sense of curiosity.

To celebrate the end of the unit, you'll reveal Rasheed's blueprints announcing a massive construction project: Vowel Town! Using a set of blueprints, students will work in rug clubs to read and write words featuring vowel teams. Then, they'll draw and label these words to create a large map of Vowel Town, featuring words like *lighthouse*, *school*, *town hall*, *train tracks*, *Main Street*, and *restaurant*. You'll want to consider the materials you can provide to give this culminating project some added flair, perhaps offering word builders colored paper, fancy markers, pastels, and glue to collage their drawings together to create a large-scale map. You might even link this work to your social studies work and design a 3-D map using cardboard or building blocks. In either case, you'll want to make this final celebration memorable, encouraging children to carry this learning forward. "Today is the last day of our unit," you'll say, "but you'll be a word builder forever and ever! You can build new words with parts you know, like vowel teams, to get the job done whenever you read and write!"

Have fun,
Havilah, Elizabeth, and Jennifer

SESSION 12

OI and *OY:* Two Vowel Teams, One Sound

GETTING READY

✔ Prepare baggies of word cards for *join, destroy, boiling, enjoy,* for each rug club.

✔ Before class, prop up Rasheed on a table by the meeting area with a blue marker under his arm and a sheet of paper next to him.

✔ Display and prepare to add to your "Vowel Teams" linking chart.

✔ Be sure students have their whiteboards and markers.

✔ Students will need their writing folders and editing pens.

PHONICS INSTRUCTION

Phonological Awareness
- Hear and connect rhyming words.

Phonics
- Distinguish between two vowel patterns that make the same sound: *OI* and *OY*.
- Recognize and use *Y* as a vowel sound (*OY, AY, EY*).

Word Knowledge/Solving
- Use knowledge of vowel patterns as well as digraphs, blends, and inflected endings to write words.
- Use knowledge of long and unique vowel CVVC patterns to edit words.

High-Frequency Words
- Learn four new words: *much, such, two, who*.

IN THIS SESSION

TODAY YOU'LL teach students two new vowel teams, *OI* and *OY*, which both make the sound /oi/. You'll present examples of *OI* and *OY* words that make the same /oi/ sound, pointing out that *OI* usually appears in the middle of a word, while *OY* often shows up at the end of a word.

TODAY YOUR STUDENTS will, with your guidance, use *OY* and *OI* when writing new words, *toy* and *choice*. Expect them to say each word slowly, listen for the /oi/ sound, and use the linking chart to help them write the words. Students will peer-edit each other's writing, using what they've learned about words with vowel teams.

MINILESSON

CONNECTION

Explain that Rasheed has a blueprint of his next project to build something new and if students want to help him, they'll need to fill up their toolbox with more vowel team parts.

As kids gathered on the rug, several of them noticed Rasheed propped up on a table next to our meeting area with a blue marker under his arm and a sheet of paper beside him. I turned to the lion. "What are you doing, Rasheed?" I asked, leaning in to listen. "You're making a blueprint? Cool!" I turned back to the class. "Blueprints are drawings or plans that help construction crews know what to build. Hmm, . . . what could Rasheed be planning to build?"

The class called out their ideas enthusiastically. "It's a big house!" "A playground?" "Is he building some really big words?" "Maybe it's a zoo! Or a school!"

"Whatever it is, I hope we can help! What do you say? Should we help Rasheed with his project?"

"Yeah!!" the class cheered back.

"What's that, Rasheed?" I once again leaned down to listen to the lion. "We can't help you?" Across the rug, faces fell. "Why not?" I listened intently, nodding my head, and turned back to the class. "Rasheed said he wishes we could help, but we're just not ready for a job *this* big. He noticed we still have a lot of empty spaces on our 'Vowel Teams' chart. So, if we want to help, he said we'll need to fill up our toolbox with more parts. We need to learn more vowel teams!

"That means we have some work to do! How many vowel teams do we have left to learn?" I turned back to the linking chart and together we counted the blank spaces. "Seven!! Whoa! That's a lot! It's going to take us *forever* to learn all of these. Hmm, . . . I wonder if we could speed things up by learning not just one, but *two* vowel teams today. Do you think you can do it?"

"Yes!!" the class called back.

❖ **Name the teaching point.**

"Today I want to teach you that *two* different vowel teams can make the same sound. *OI* and *OY* make the sound /oi/."

TEACHING

Present examples of how the vowel teams *OI* and *OY* appear in words, such as *coin* and *boy*, and make the same sound /oi/. Point out how *OI* is usually in the middle of a word and *OY* often appears at the end of a word.

"How handy! Even though we have to remember two different teams, we only have to remember *one* new sound. Both *OI* and *OY* make the sound /oi/. But here's a tip. When you read and write, you usually find these vowel teams in different places in a word. *OI* will almost always be in the middle of a word and *OY* will almost always be at the end of a word. Let me show you what I mean."

I wrote the word *coin* on a piece of chart paper, and we read it together. I then quickly wrote the letters *OI* under the word on the easel. "Say /oi/ when I point to this vowel team," I said, pointing under the letters *OI*. "Now let's read this word again." I ran my finger under the word *coin* as the class read the word together.

 coin

 oi

"The vowel team *OI* makes the sound /oi/ in the middle of the word *coin*. You can see the vowel team *OI* in the middle, too.

"Now let's study another word with the same sound /oi/." I wrote the word *boy* next to the word *coin*.

"Read this word with me." I then wrote the letters *OY* under the word *boy*. "Say /oi/ when I point to this vowel team," I said, pointing under the letters *OY*. "Now let's read this word again." I ran my finger under the word *boy* as the class read the word together.

SESSION 12: *OI* AND *OY*: TWO VOWEL TEAMS, ONE SOUND

FIG. 12–1 Rasheed with his blueprints.

Of course, there are exceptions to this generalization in words such as royal, voyage, *and* oyster, *but most of the words your readers encounter in their texts will follow this principle. Make sure to keep your language tentative and if an exception comes up, celebrate the observation.*

boy

oy

"This time, I hear the /oi/ sound at the end of the word. Say it slowly and listen for the /oi/. Do you hear it?" Children nodded their heads. "But this time that sound is being made by the letters *OY*. This will be so helpful when you want to write a word with an /oi/ sound. If you hear that sound in the *middle* of the word, like *coin*, then use the letters *OI*. But if you hear the sound at the end of the word, like *boy*, then you can use the letters *OY*.

"Let's add these to our linking chart to remind us of what we've learned. I'll write the words here, and we can add the pictures later." I quickly added the team *OI* and the word *coin* to the next box in the class linking chart. Then I added the team *OY* and the word *boy*. We read the two words before moving on.

ACTIVE ENGAGEMENT/ LINK

Work with students to use *OY* and *OI* in writing new words, *toy* and *choice*. Remind them to say each word slowly, listening for the /oi/ sound, and use the linking chart to help choose *OY* or *OI* as they write the words.

"Are you ready to try using these new vowel teams? Let's pretend for a minute that we are in writing workshop." I readied myself with a pretend pen and paper in front of me. "I'm writing a story about the time I was choosing a birthday present for my niece. I want to write the word *toy*, because I was trying to pick a *toy* she would like best.

"With your partner, say the word slowly together, listen for where you hear the sound /oi/, then use the linking chart to help you decide. Do you need an *OI* or *OY* to spell this word? Turn and work with your partner. Write it down on your whiteboard." I listened in as partners stretched the word *toy*, listening for the placement of the sound and then indicating the vowel team they would use.

"I heard many of you say I need to use the vowel team *OY* to write *toy* because you heard the sound /oi/ at the *end* of the word." I stretched the word *toooooooyyy*, emphasizing the sound at the end and wrote it on the easel. "Let's read the word *toy* together and check the vowel team," I said, running my finger under the word and pointing out the vowel team.

"Now what if I kept writing my story about picking out a present for my niece and I wanted to write the word *choice*? I thought she would like both of the toys I'd picked out, but I had to make a *choice* because I could only get her one.

"Again, say the word slowly together, listen for where you hear the sound /oi/, then use the linking chart to help you decide. Do you need an *OI* or *OY* to spell this word? Turn and work with your partner to spell the word *choice*. Write it on your whiteboard." I listened in as partners stretched the word out, thinking about where they heard the /oi/ sound and then selecting the vowel team to use.

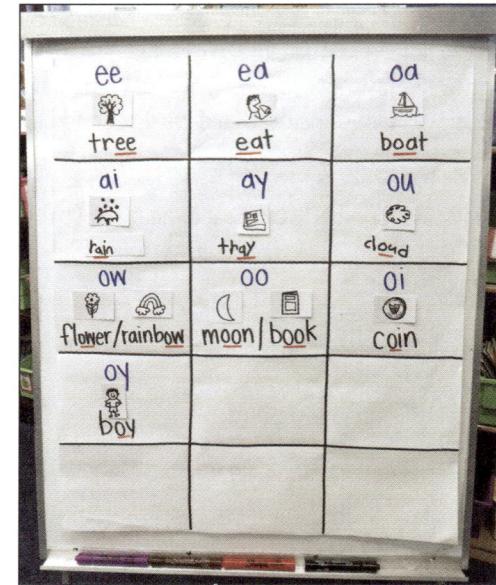

FIG. 12–2 Adding two new vowel teams to the class chart.

Just so you know, one of the jobs of Silent E is to alert the reader that C or G is making a soft sound like in choice *and* page. *This isn't something you'll want to get into with your kids right now. If a child spells* choice *with an S, simply point out that in this word, the sound /s/ is made by the letter* C.

RUG TIME (CLUBS)

Channel children to work with clubmates to figure out how to spell new *OI* and *OY* words.

"Let's keep this writing workshop help going, word builders," I said as I distributed a baggie of four words to each club, including the words *join*, *destroy*, *boiling*, and *enjoy*.

"There are four words in your baggie. Each word contains one of the new vowel teams we learned today. Everyone, choose one word card from the baggie. Then, use what you learned about *OI* and *OY* to help you read your word. Remember, both teams make the sound /oi/. Keep your word card facedown so nobody else can peek at it." I waited for members of each rug club to do so.

"Now, take turns being the reader and the writers. The reader will read his or her word out loud without showing his or her card. Then, the writers will listen closely and spell it the best they can. Remember writers, you'll want to listen up for where you hear /oi/—in the middle of the word or at the end? Study the linking chart to help you remember where you'll usually find *OI* and where you'll usually find *OY*.

"Then the reader will show you his or her word, so you can check and see if your spelling matches. If you need to, fix up the word. Get started!" As children worked, I moved from one group to the next, coaching writers as they isolated the vowel sound /oi/, suggesting that they use the linking chart to help decide whether to use *OI* or *OY* to spell the word.

join	destroy
boiling	enjoy

SHARE • Peer-Editing to Fix Up Tough Words

Partners peer-edit with pieces from their writing folders using the "Vowel Team" chart.

"Word builders, I bet there are words in your writing that could use this same kind of careful looking and listening and checking and fixing up.

"Let's use our 'Vowel Teams' chart in a new way—to edit pieces in your writing folder, going back to fix up tough words. Instead of fixing your own writing, you'll fix your partner's writing. You can reread a piece written by your partner, listening for vowel sounds and checking for words that don't look right. Our chart can help you choose the team that might help you get the job done.

"Right now, swap your whiteboards for your writing folder and pen." I waited a moment for kids to do so.

"Partner 1, take out a piece of writing you have been working on. Partner 2, can you put your editor glasses on and help your partner take a closer look at words with vowel teams? Also, be sure to listen up for vowel sounds as you read. When you hear sounds like /ē/ or /ou/ or /oi/, stop and check that you used the right letters to make that sound. If you find any words that don't quite look right, you can use our 'Vowel Teams' chart to try those words another way."

EXTENSION 1 • Learning New Snap Words that Rhyme:
Much, Such, Two, Who

 GETTING READY

- Gather snap word cards for *much*, *such*, *two*, and *who*. Prepare to display them on the easel.
- Display your "Make it a SNAP word!" anchor chart.

Play a word game with students—ask them to find the rhyming pairs.

"Let's play a little game. I have four words in my hand. See if you can find the rhyming pairs. Are you ready? Listen closely, word builders!" I held the words to myself, not letting kids see them yet, but just listing them out loud.

"*Much, two, who, such,*" I said slowly. "Thumbs up if you heard the rhyming pairs." A few thumbs appeared along the rug. I said the words one more time and more students indicated they had found the pairs. "I think you heard the rhymes. *Much* and *such* sound the same, and *two* and *who* rhyme."

Challenge children to find two words that rhyme and have the same word part, -uch. Point out that *two* and *who* end with the same vowel, O. Then ask partners to make sentences using the four new snap words.

"The great thing about these words is that they are pretty easy to learn." I placed all four words on the edge of the easel. "Two of them have the same word part in them, which makes them sound the same and look similar. Will you read them with me and spot the two that rhyme and have the same word part?"

We read all four words together. "*Much* and *such*!" kids called out as they noticed both words had the same ending, *-uch*.

"And *two* and *who* end with the same vowel." I pointed to the letter *O* at the end of each word.

"Let's practice them in pairs," I said, pointing to our snap word chart. "Get ready to turn *much* and *such* into snap words."

Together, we went through each step. When we got to the last step, I asked Partner 1 to think of a sentence for the word *much* and Partner 2 to think of one for *such* and share with each other before adding both words to the class word wall. Then we repeated the steps for *two* and *who*.

EXTENSION 2 • Watching Out for Vowels that Team Up with Y (AY, OY, EY)

GETTING READY
- Display your "Vowel Teams" chart.

Guide students to think about how EY works in words like *key*.

"Reading words like *boy* and *joy* today reminded me of what we know about *Y* at the end of words. You know that *Y* can make a lot of different sounds at the end of a word, like the /ē/ sound in *candy*, or the /ī/ sound in the word *my*.

"Here's a little tip to help you read words that end with a *Y*. Look and see if there is a vowel teaming up with the *Y*. This gives you a clue about the sound *Y* might be making.

"For example, you already know that if there's an *A* teaming up with *Y* . . ." I pointed to the vowel team chart, "this usually makes an /ā/ sound, like in the word *play*. And today you learned that if there's an *O* teaming up with the *Y*, then this team makes an /oi/ sound like in the words *joy* and *destroy* and *boy*!" I said, pointing once again to our "Vowel Teams" chart.

"Here's one more vowel that likes to team up with the vowel *Y*." I wrote *EY* on the easel. "If you ever see an *E* teaming up with a *Y*, that's a clue that the *Y* is usually going to make an /ē/ sound. Let's play a little game with some *EY* words. I'm going to write a word on the easel. Will you whisper to your partner and see if you can figure out how to read it? Keep it a secret and don't call it out. When you know what the word is, stand up and act it out!

"Let's try one together. Remember not to call it out if you know it!" I wrote the word *key* on the easel. "I know *EY* usually says /ē/, so this word must be /k/-/eeeee/, *key*!" I said in a loud whisper, pretending to be keeping a secret. "Now let's stand up and act it out. Think about how you'll do this. Ready, go!" Soon everyone was turning their hands as if they were opening a door or starting a car with a key in their hands.

Rally children to play a game to act out words that end in *-ey*, like *hockey* or *turkey*.

"Sit back down, and let's start the game." I turned to the easel and wrote the word *hockey*. After some excited whispers between partners, the class was soon once again on their feet practicing some slap shots with their imaginary hockey sticks. "What's this word?" I asked, pointing to the easel.

"*Hockey*!" the class shouted out.

"Right! Back in your spots. Here's round two!" We continued in this manner, reading and acting out the words *monkey*, *honey*, *donkey*, *money*, and *turkey*.

Session 13

Helpful Clues for Vowel Teams *EW* and *UE*

GETTING READY

✔ Before class, put Rasheed on a chair. Print out his letter and his poem and put both in your copy of *Tumbleweed Stew*, along with a Post-it with the word *clue* written on it. Put the book on the easel.

✔ Write the word *stew* on two-column chart paper and continue to add words.

✔ Prepare copies of Rasheed's poem and gather highlighters for each partnership.

✔ Be ready to write *EW* and *UE* words from the poem on a two-column chart.

✔ Display and prepare to add *EW* and *UE* words and illustrations to your "Vowel Teams" linking chart.

PHONICS INSTRUCTION

Phonological Awareness
- Segment onsets and rimes.

Phonics
- Hear and identify the vowel sound in words, locating the letters that represent the sound.
- Distinguish between two vowel patterns that make the same sound: *EW* and *UE*.
- Recognize and use letter combinations that represent unique vowel sounds to decode words with a CVVC pattern.

High-Frequency Words
- Learn one new word: *few*.
- Review and recognize snap words with automaticity.

IN THIS SESSION

TODAY YOU'LL teach students two new vowel teams, *EW* and *UE*, which usually make the sound /o͞o/, like in the words *stew* and *blue*.

TODAY YOUR STUDENTS will listen to and look closely at *EW* and *EU* words that make the same /o͞o/ sound. Expect them to use their knowledge of *EW* and *EU* vowel teams to figure out how to read in a familiar shared reading text with more words, such as *crew* and *rescue*.

MINILESSON

CONNECTION

Read aloud a letter from Rasheed urging the class to learn two new vowel teams that make the /o͞o/ sound.

As students gathered on the rug I glanced at the easel, feigning surprise. "What's this doing here?" I asked, pointing to the copy of *Tumbleweed Stew* propped on the ledge of the easel. "I didn't leave that there. It looks like there's a note!" I held up the book with a piece of paper sticking out the top and a Post-it with the word *clue* stuck to the front.

"It's a clue! Open it! Let's see!" A chorus of voices prompted me.

"Okay. Okay." I picked up the copy of the text and read the letter (see Figure 13–1) to the class.

"Let's not waste another minute, Word Builders." I placed page 3 under the document camera. "Rasheed said we need to listen up for words that make the same vowel sound as *school*. So we need to listen for the vowel sound . . ."

"/oo̅/!" kids chimed in.

"And then we need to look closely for the new vowel teams that make the sound /oo̅/. Hold up your hand and stop me when you notice the teams. Here we go." We started reading together. When we got to the line, "The sky is blue," a few hands popped up.

"Did some of you hear an /oo̅/ sound in this word?" I asked, pointing under the word *blue*. "Let's read it again, listening for the sound."

"*Bluuuue*," we said together slowly.

"Yup, I hear the sound /oo̅/. But I *see* the vowels *U* and *E*. This must be the first team Rasheed wants us to learn! Let's keep reading to see if we can find the second vowel team." We continued on until the word *stew* on the next line. More hands went up this time. Once again, we reread the word slowly, listening for the /oo̅/ sound in *stew*, this time identifying the *EW* vowel team.

♣ **Name the teaching point.**

"Today I want to remind you that different vowel teams can make the same sound. *EW* and *UE* make the sound /oo̅/, like in the words *stew* and *blue*."

TEACHING

Guide children to study *stew* and *blue* to see the vowel teams in isolation.

"Rasheed left us two words as clues to learn about the vowel teams *EW* and *UE*. Let's take a closer look at these two teams."

I wrote the word *stew* on a piece of two-column chart paper. I pointed to the word, saying, "Read it with me."

"*Stew!*" the class called out.

"Yes! At the end of this word you can see the letters for this new vowel team, *E* and *W*, side by side. Let's double-check the sound it makes." I quickly drew two Elkonin boxes on a small whiteboard.

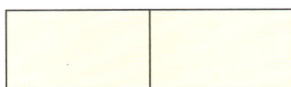

Dear Word Builders,

I really need your help with my project, but there are more vowel teams for you to learn. Here's a clue to help you build your vowel team chart:

> Read page 3 and you will see two new teams. They make the same sound as /oo/ like in **school**, but they LOOK completely different.

Can you find them?

Your friend,
Rasheed

FIG. 13–1 Rasheed leaves a clue behind to reveal two new vowel teams.

SESSION 13: HELPFUL CLUES FOR VOWEL TEAMS *EW* AND *UE*

"Will you say the word *stew* slowly as I push the sounds into each box?" As the class stretched the word *stew*, I moved my index finger into the box that corresponded with each sound. "I'm hearing the blend /st/, and the sound /o͞o/." I wrote the letters into the boxes.

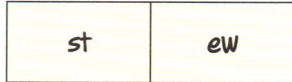

"The vowel team *EW* makes the sound /o͞o/. Say /o͞o/ when I point to this vowel team," I said, pointing under the letters *EW*. "Now let's read this word again." I ran my finger under the word *stew* as the class read the word together.

Then I wrote the word *blue* on the other side of the chart paper. "We also found another vowel team that makes the sound /o͞o/. Read this word with me." I pointed to *blue*.

"*Blue*!" the class called out.

"Yes! At the end of this word you can see this new vowel team, *U* and *E*, side by side. Let's double-check the sound it makes." I quickly drew two Elkonin boxes on a small whiteboard.

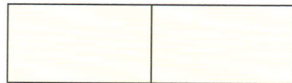

"Will you say the word *blue* slowly as I push the sounds into each box?" As the class stretched the word *blue*, I moved my index finger into the box that corresponded with each sound. "I'm hearing the blend, /bl/, and the sound /o͞o/." I wrote the letters into the boxes.

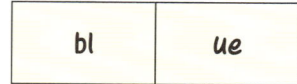

"The vowel team *UE* also makes the sound /o͞o/. Say /o͞o/ when I point to this vowel team," I said, pointing under the letters *UE*. "Now let's read this word again." I ran my finger under the word *blue* as the class read the word together.

"The vowel teams *EW*, like in the word *stew*, and *UE*, like in the word *blue*, both make the sound /o͞o/. Our toolbox of vowel teams is really growing, word builders. We are getting close to being able to help Rasheed with his project, but before we add these two new teams to our 'Vowel Teams' chart, I think we need more practice. We need to see how these teams work in other words."

Typically when using Elkonin boxes, you would draw one box for each sound. In this case, you could draw three boxes, one for the S, one for the T and one for the EW. We chose to keep the ST together to support children in seeing these letters as a word part.

FIG. 13–2 Studying words with the vowel teams EW and UE.

We recognize that sometimes EW makes the sound /ū/ as in the word few. However, in most of the words your students encounter, these vowel teams will make an /o͞o/ sound, as in grew and flew. The sounds are close enough that trying the /o͞o/ sound, and then thinking about what makes sense, should help readers get to the alternate /ū/ sound when necessary.

ACTIVE ENGAGEMENT/LINK

Channel students to see how vowel teams *EW* and *UE* work in *blue* and *crew*.

"I wonder what we could do to help us practice?" I tapped my chin, as I looked around the room and then spied another piece of paper tucked inside *Tumbleweed Stew*. I pulled it out. "What's this? Wait! It seems like Rasheed wasn't just writing us clues last night. I think he was also writing . . ." I looked closely at the paper, "a love poem?" The class giggled.

"Let's see if our new vowel teams can help us read this love poem Rasheed left us. Can you be on the lookout for any words with the new vowel teams *EW* and *UE*?" I pointed to the two teams in the words *stew* and *blue* written on the easel. "Remember, both words make the vowel sound /o͞o/. I bet these will really help us figure out Rasheed's poem."

I placed the paper under the document camera, revealing just the first stanza. We began reading together, stopping at the word *blue*. "It's this word again! Say it slowly to your partner. Remind them what sound the *UE* is making." I gave students a brief moment to confirm the sound with their partners.

"Let's reread this and keep going. Will you put your hand out to tell me when we get to another word with *UE* or *EW*?" We read to the end of the first stanza, stopping once again to have partners check the sound of *EW* in the word *crew*.

"These new vowel teams are really helpful! So far, this poem has two words with the vowel sound /o͞o/, *blue* and *crew*.

RUG TIME

Challenge partners to find more *EW* and *UE* words in Rasheed's poem.

"Poor Rasheed, it sounds like he really needs our help. Let's read the rest of this poem. I'll give each partnership a copy of the poem and you can work together as a rug club to read it. Be on the lookout for the vowel teams *EW* and *UE*. If you spot them in a word, remember that both teams make the sound /o͞o/. You can use these teams to help you read the words. Highlight these words or circle them with a pen when you find them. You might also notice other vowel teams in words. Use *everything* you know to help you get this job done.

"Let's go, let's go . . ." I began singing as I passed out copies of the poem and a highlighter to each partnership.

"It's time to work. Let's go!" the class called back as they got to work. As students began reading, I circulated among the group, coaching as needed.

FIG. 13–3 Rasheed's poem

By stopping to double-check this known word, you are modeling the close looking you hope your students will be doing. You want them to be aware of features they have learned, noticing familiar words or word parts in new contexts. While in reading workshop, you're likely to be emphasizing fluency and encouraging children to move on if they see a familiar word. It's okay to slow this work down during your phonics instruction.

SHARE • Reviewing and Recording *EW* and *UE* Words

Reread the poem together. Then point out all words with *EW* and *UE* from the poem, adding them to the appropriate column on the chart paper.

"Let's read the whole poem all together." We quickly did a shared reading of the text. "It's a good thing we learned two new vowel teams again today, because now we are even closer to being ready to help Rasheed with his project, and it really sounds like he wants our help.

"Can you share the words you found as you were reading the poem? Let's add some more words to our collection for the vowel teams *EW* and *UE*." I turned back to the chart paper where I had written the words *stew* and *blue* earlier. "In the first part of the poem we noticed the word *crew*. Let's add that word to the chart. Will you say it slowly while I write it down? Listen for the vowel sound /o͞o/." We stretched the word as I wrote it down. Then I had students call out the rest of the words they found as I recorded them on the chart.

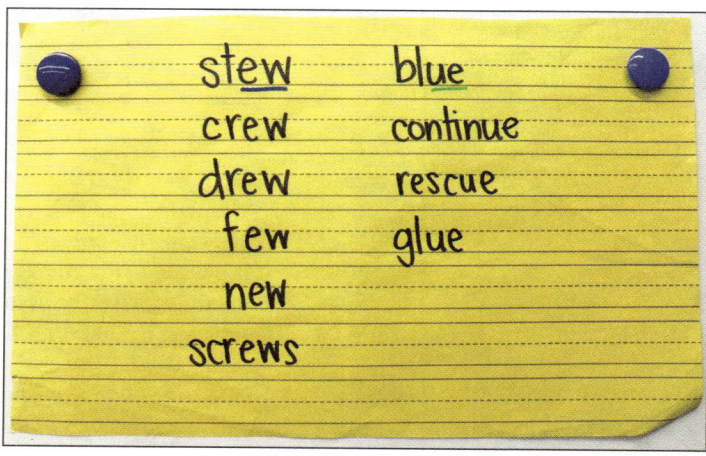

FIG. 13–4 Sorting words with *EW* and *UE*.

Choose one word to represent each team on the "Vowel Teams" linking chart.

"Now we have lots of words to choose from to add to the chart. Some of these words are a little tricky to remember with pictures, so I'm going to choose *screw* and *glue*. These are also helpful construction materials." I added the words to the chart with a quick illustration.

POSSIBLE COACHING MOVES

▸ "You noticed a word with *EW*. Say it slowly. Listen to the sound it's making. Yes! It's an /o͞o/ sound! Highlight it!"

▸ "Do you know another word that looks like that? This first part looks like *car*. Let me write that on a Post-it for you. If this says *car* . . . then this says . . . *par*! Now add the ending. Yes, *parts*! Read that line again and check that it makes sense."

▸ "Try the vowels another way. Does it make sense?"

▸ "Can you break that word into parts? Read the first part (*con*). Read the next part (*tin*). Now read the last part—it's a vowel team! Put it all together. Does the word *continue* make sense? Yes!"

Again, don't feel that it's necessary to be limited to these examples. If you have an Andrew *in your classroom, point out the vowel team and add his name to your chart instead!*

EXTENSION 1 • Adding to Your High-Frequency Word Bank: Learning the Word *Few*

GETTING READY

- Display Rasheed's poem.
- Be sure kids have their whiteboards.
- Display the "Make it a SNAP word!" anchor chart.
- Be ready to add the word card for *few* on the word wall.

Rally partners to make *few* into a snap word.

"As we read Rasheed's poem I noticed a word that comes up quite often in our reading and writing. It's the word *few*. Let's go back and find that word." I placed the poem back under the document camera and together we read the last two lines of the second stanza.

> A few new vowel teams,
>
> and then they can start.

I pointed under the word *few* in the text. "This word says . . ."

"*Few*!" the class called out.

"Word builders, you know what to do! I don't think you need an adult to help you turn this word into a snap word, do you? Work together with your partner, going through each step on our 'Make it a SNAP word!' chart.

You'll know you're ready when you can both read and write this word in a snap! Help each other out and see if you can do it before our time is up. Be ready to share anything interesting you noticed as you studied this word. If you're waiting for other people to finish up, work with your partner to practice some of the other words on our word wall."

"Let's go, let's go . . ." We began singing as students grabbed their materials and got started. After a little time to work, I called them together, inviting anyone to share what they noticed about the word.

"It's only three letters," said Eva. "That makes it easy to learn."

"It's a little different from the other *EW* words," noted Alex. "This one sounds more like /ū/, not /o͞o/."

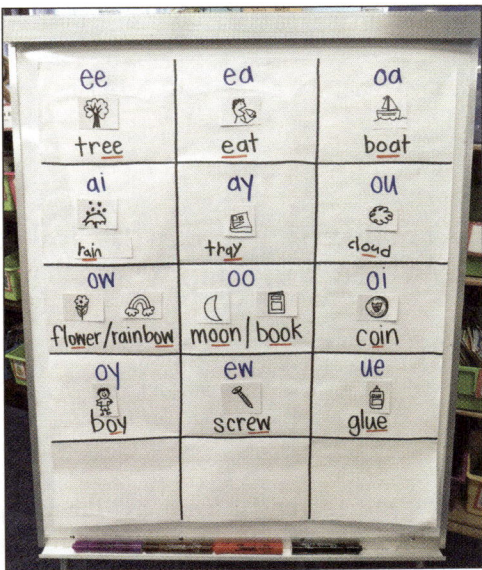

FIG. 13–5 Adding *screw* and *glue* to the "Vowel Teams" chart.

SESSION 13: HELPFUL CLUES FOR VOWEL TEAMS *EW* AND *UE*

"It looks just like the word *new*!" said Ahmed. "I read that word in one of my books."

We then chanted the letters one more time, giving a big cheer for our new word as I added the word card to our word wall.

EXTENSION 2 • Pay the Toll to Cross the Bridge: Noticing the Vowel Team in Snap Words

 GETTING READY

- Have your snap word cards for words with vowel teams ready to show students to play this game. You could use words such as *down*, *school*, *away*, *about*, *been*, *easy*, *each*, *few*, *house*, *know*, *wait*, and other words.

As students line up for lunch, ask them to play a game in which they read a snap word and then tell you another word with the same vowel team.

"Today, as you walk past me to line up for lunch, let's pretend you have to cross over a bridge to get to the lunch line. But before you can cross the bridge, you'll need to pay the toll. To pay today's toll, you have to read a snap word that I hold up. Then look carefully at the vowels in that word and tell me another word with the same vowel team. Tyvell, you're first!" I held up a snap word card.

"*Down*!" shouted Tyvell.

"And another word with the same vowel team is . . ."

"*Town*!" he filled in.

"Ching, ching! That works. You can cross the bridge."

"Now, Sara, it's your turn. If Sara is stuck, we can give her some hints. Here's the next word!" I held out the snap word *school*. "If you need help thinking of another word with that vowel team, try thinking of one that rhymes."

The kids quickly continued crossing the bridge, as I displayed the snap words with vowel teams such as *away*, *about*, *been*, *easy*, *each*, *few*, *house*, *know*, and *wait*. I offered coaching and hints as needed. The children cheered as each child crossed the bridge. "All of you made it to the other side! Lunch time!"

SESSION 14

Word Builders Look Out and Listen Up to Use the Right Vowel Team

IN THIS SESSION

TODAY YOU'LL teach students to pay close attention to vowel teams because they can sound the same but look different. You'll work with kids to interactively write a new warning sign about vowel teams.

TODAY YOUR STUDENTS will practice using vowel teams that sound the same but look different. Students will apply their vowel team knowledge to edit their writing pieces from writing workshop.

GETTING READY

- ✔ Display your "Vowel Teams" chart.
- ✔ You'll need chart paper and markers for interactive writing. When you're done, hang up the new sign.
- ✔ Be sure kids have whiteboards and markers.
- ✔ Children will need their writing folders and editing pens.

MINILESSON

CONNECTION

Tell children a story about mixing up tools to build a bookcase, choosing the wrong one for the job. Relate that to mixing up vowel teams.

I sat down in the meeting area and signaled for kids to gather quickly. "Word builders, last night I was putting together some new bookshelves with my sister. We had our toolbox out and we were following the directions really carefully." I mimed lugging a heavy toolbox over toward my chair and opening a set of instructions. "We were working together just like a real construction crew.

"When we were ready to screw the top of the bookshelf to the sides, my sister called out, 'Hand me a screwdriver!' So I reached inside the toolbox and grabbed one. But when she tried to use it, guess what? It didn't work!" I explained, "It was the wrong kind of screwdriver. I hadn't looked closely to find the right one for the job.

"I'm telling you this because vowel teams are easy to mix up, too. If you're not careful you might use the wrong one."

PHONICS INSTRUCTION

Phonics
- Consolidate learning by writing CVVC words with the vowel teams *OI/OY*, *EW/UE*, *OU/OW*, *AY/AI*, *EA/EE*.
- Hear and identify the vowel sound in words, locating the letters that represent the sound.
- Distinguish between two vowel patterns that make the same sound.

Word Knowledge/Solving
- Use knowledge of long and unique vowel CVVC patterns to edit words.

High-Frequency Words
- Review and recognize snap words with automaticity.

❖ **Name the teaching point.**

"Today I want to teach you that word builders need to *look out* and *listen up* when they read and write with vowel teams. You'll need to pay attention because vowel teams can sound the same, but look different."

TEACHING AND ACTIVE ENGAGEMENT/LINK

Invite children to share tips about vowel teams that are important to remember as they write. Then suggest how they might write a warning sign for writing workshop.

"This is an important warning. Vowel teams can get all mixed up if you're not careful! I think we need to make another warning sign for our construction zone! Oh wait, I mean our classroom! We already have a warning for reading workshop," I pointed to the interactive writing from the first bend, "reminding us to watch out for vowel teams that don't work the same way like *AI* in *said* and *EE* in *been*.

"I think we need a warning sign for writing workshop! What could this warning sign remind us about vowel teams? What is important for us to remember as we write? Turn and teach each other a few important tips for using vowel teams."

After a moment, I brought the class back together. "I heard so many helpful tips about vowel teams. What if our warning sign said something like this."

> **Vowels join** together to make **new** teams and new **sounds**.
> BUT . . . **pay** attention!
> Some vowel **teams** sound the same but look different.

Kids nodded in agreement. "Let's get started, word builders, there's no time to waste. Get your whiteboards and markers." Kids readied their tools as I clipped a new sheet of chart paper to the easel and made sure the class vowel team chart was hanging in view.

Ask kids to try writing the first word for the sign, *vowels*, reminding them to think about which vowel team to use, *OW* or *OU*.

"Our first word is *vowels*. Listen up! What sound do you hear in the middle of the word *vowels*?" We stretched the word together, "*Vowwwwels*. Yes, you hear /ou/. There's a vowel team working to make that sound. Do you think *OW* is making that sound or *OU*?" I gestured toward the "Vowel Teams" chart. "Quickly, write the word both ways and decide which one looks right."

Students used their whiteboards to write the word both ways, *vowels* and *vouels*. Then I helped them identify which word looked right. "Yes, the word *vowels* uses the vowel team *OW*." I quickly found a student who had spelled the word correctly on her board and asked her to come up and write *vowels* on our sign.

As you listen to kids' suggestions for interactive writing, you might capture some of the words kids use, especially listening for words with vowel teams.

Rather than calling on kids to share their ideas aloud, it helps to voice back what you "heard partners say," using a pre-planned text, like the one we provide here. You'll notice that we incorporated keywords that feature easily confused vowel teams like EA and EE, AI and AY, OW and OU and EW and UE to give kids lots of opportunities to practice listening for and recording these vowel sounds.

Many first-graders won't necessarily know which way looks right when trying out the spelling of a word. Focus less on being "right" and more on developing the habit of trying words out a couple different ways, picking the best one and moving on. This is a practice you want them to take on with independence during writing workshop. "If you're doing this on your own," you might say, "you won't always know which way looks right. That's okay. Pick the best one and use it in your writing. You can always circle the word and come back to check it later."

Continue sharing the pen to write the rest of the warning sign, asking children to choose vowel teams that might be confused with another vowel team, such as *OI/OY, EW/UE, OU/OW, AI/AY*, and *EA/EE*.

We worked through the rest of the message, sharing the pen for the words containing vowel teams that could be confused with another team, including *join*, *new*, *sounds*, *pay*, and *teams*. Each time we got to one of those words I encouraged students to first listen for the vowel sound, then try it two ways before selecting the one that looked right.

After finishing the last line, I paused the class and said, "Good thing we're making this sign together. It will remind us when we write to *listen up* and *look out* for vowel teams and pay attention because even when vowel teams sound the same, they look different."

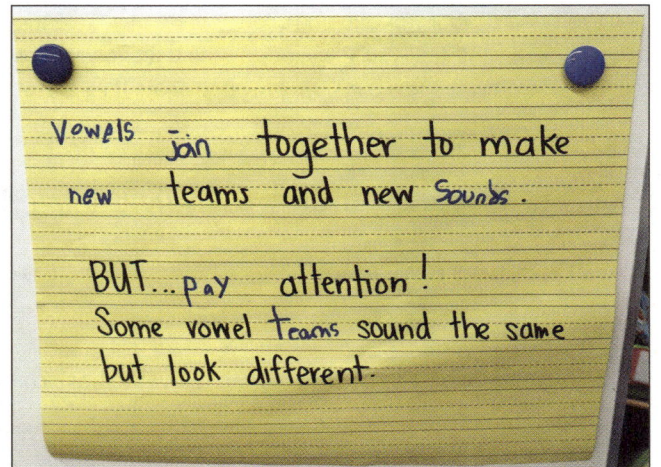

RUG TIME

Channel partners to edit their writing workshop pieces, looking out and listening up for vowel teams as they edit. Post the new interactive warning sign and remind kids to refer to it.

"Instead of waiting until writing workshop, let's put this sign to good use right now! Quick! Take out your editing pen and your writing folders. Pull out one of your pieces. Work with your partner to look out and listen up for vowel teams, especially teams that sound the same, like *AY* and *AI*, *EW* and *UE*, and *OU* and *OW!*" I pointed to each team on the class linking chart.

"If you hear one of these vowel sounds, check to make sure the word looks right. If not, work with your partner to try it a few different ways and decide which one looks the way it would in a book. Then, switch to edit your partner's piece. While you get started, I'll hang up our warning sign nearby, so we'll remember to pay attention when we use vowel teams to spell." I posted the class interactive writing beside the first warning sign we had cowritten. Then, I moved from one partnership to another, coaching students to listen for vowels as they checked their words.

SHARE • Making Good Moves to Fix Up Vowel Teams and Edit Writing

Compliment writers on all the good moves they're making with vowel teams as they edit their writing. Then ask partners to share the writing they edited with their rug club.

"Writers, you are unstoppable! You are listening up for those vowel sounds as you reread your words and looking out for the letters you used to spell. I see you looking up at the 'Vowel Teams' chart to help you check what part might make that sound, trying it more than one way to fix up your words.

Expect approximations as writers edit. Kids will likely add vowel teams where they don't belong or confuse vowel teams that make the same (or similar) sounds. Use your observations to help you plan for small groups during writing workshop.

SESSION 14: WORD BUILDERS LOOK OUT AND LISTEN UP TO USE THE RIGHT VOWEL TEAM

"Will you turn to your rug club and show a place in your writing that you and your partner fixed up? Or, instead, you might show a word that you spelled using the right vowel team!" I prompted partners to share with the other half of their rug club, giving them a minute or two to share their edits.

EXTENSION 1 • Adding to Individualized "Vowel Teams" Charts

GETTING READY

- Make sure children have their own "Vowel Teams" charts from Session 6, Extension 1.

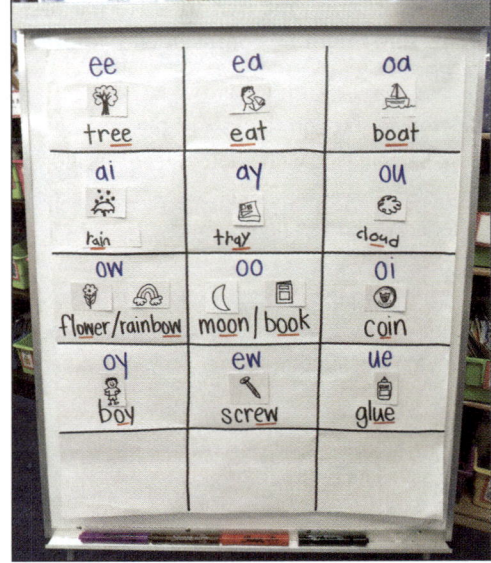

Invite partners to add to their personal "Vowel Teams" charts to help solve tough words in their own books.

During reading workshop, I signaled for the class's attention. "Readers, I just walked past our warning sign and realized that this reminder is important not only when you use vowel teams to write, but also when you use vowel teams to read! You need to look out for those parts and remember the sound a part usually makes.

"Take out your 'Vowel Teams' chart and fill it up like a toolbox, with all the new parts you can use to solve words." Pointing to the class chart, I suggested, "Check our class chart to help you fill in the vowel teams we've studied recently. Then, add a word that uses that vowel team and draw a picture to match! Remember, you can always use the same words we chose together or another word you know really well."

I circulated, coaching in as children added an anchor word, or two, for each vowel team, reminding them about the multiple sounds of vowel teams like *OW* and *OO*. Once children finished updating their chart, I reminded them to use this tool whenever they read.

EXTENSION 2 • Shining a Light on Snap Words

 GETTING READY

- Have a flashlight ready to highlight words on the word wall.

Invite children to play a game they know to review and write snap words.

I dimmed the lights and got out a flashlight. Kids clapped their hands in excitement as we got ready for a flashlight word wall hunt. "It's time to make sure those snap words are sharp in your mind, so you'll be ready to scoop them up when you read, put them down on the page quickly when you write, and use them to help you read *and* write new words.

"Remember, I'll shine a flashlight on a word on our word wall, and you shout out that word. Are you ready?"

I directed the flashlight up toward the ceiling. "You know the chant. Are you ready?" I started snapping my fingers and chanting to the beat as kids joined in:

> I'm looking for a snap word, a snap word, a snap word
> I'm looking for a snap word to make bright!
> I'm looking for a snap word, a snap word, a snap word
> I'm looking for a snap word to shine my *light*!

My flashlight illuminated the word *away*. Two or three kids shouted, "*Away*!" Then I said, "Let's spell it like we are cheering! Give me an *A*!" The kids chimed back with *A*. Then I continued through the letters.

Passing the flashlight to a student, I said, "Now Frankie's going to find a word! Everyone start chanting!" I whispered for Frankie to start with the light on the ceiling, and then bring it down. I led the class in the same chant. Frankie's light landed on *near*.

The students shouted, "*Near*!" I again led them in a chant, this time starting with "Give me an *N*!"

SESSION 15

Adding to Our Toolbox: Vowel Teams *AW* and *AU*

GETTING READY

✓ For each rug club, prepare a baggie of *AW* and *AU* words: *crawl*, *straw*, *drawing*, *yawning*, *faucet*, *launch*, *laundry*, *haunted*.

✓ Be ready to write *saw* and *pause* on chart paper.

✓ Be sure students have whiteboards and markers.

✓ Prepare word cards for *saw*, *claw*, *hawk*, *haul*, and *fault* and place in a pocket chart.

✓ Prepare to add new *AW* and *AU* words and illustrations to your "Vowel Teams" linking chart.

PHONICS INSTRUCTION

Concepts About Print
- Use language conventions to write a sentence, including capitals and end punctuation.

Phonological Awareness
- Isolate and pronounce initial, medial vowel, and ending sounds in spoken single-syllable words.
- Change the beginning, ending, or middle phoneme to make a new word.

Phonics
- Hear and identify the vowel sound in words, locating the letters that represent the sound.

- Distinguish between two vowel patterns that make the same sound: *AW* and *AU*.
- Recognize and use letter combinations that represent unique vowel sounds to build and decode words with a CVVC pattern.

High-Frequency Words
- Learn one new high-frequency word: *because*.
- Spell high-frequency words with automaticity.

IN THIS SESSION

TODAY YOU'LL teach students that when they hear the /ô/ sound in a word, it's usually made by the vowel teams *AW* or *AU*. You'll guide children to listen closely to *AW* and *AU* words and act them out.

TODAY YOUR STUDENTS will build some new words with *AW* and *AU* vowel teams. Expect them to listen to words in sentences, say and write the words, act them out, and make new words that are similar.

MINILESSON

CONNECTION

Tell children little bits of a story. Invite them to predict what happens next by giving them sound clues, *OW* and *Awwwww*. Highlight the importance of listening carefully to vowel teams.

"Let's play a game. I'm going to tell you just a little bit of a story, and you make a prediction and tell me what happens next. Ready? I was walking down the street on a bright sunny day, when all of a sudden, I said, '*OW*!'" I paused and looked at the class. "What do you think happened?"

Kids called out guesses, "You got stung by a bee!" "You stubbed your toe!" "Somebody pinched you!"

I smiled. "Any of those would make sense! Here's the beginning of another little story . . . I was walking down the street on a bright sunny day, when all of a sudden I said, '*Awwwwww*!' What do you think happened this time?"

"You saw a little dog!" "Somebody gave you flowers!" "You saw a cute baby!" voices called out.

"Did you notice how changing one little sound made a big difference in the story I was telling? That's why it's so important to pay careful attention to the middle of a word where you'll find a lot of vowel teams hiding. You want to make sure you use the right sound to match the letters you see."

❖ Name the teaching point.

"Today I want to teach you that when you hear that *awwwww* sound in a word, it's usually made by the vowel teams *AW* or *AU*."

TEACHING

Guide children to study *AW* and *AU* vowel teams, listening closely to how they sound and how they both make the /ô/ sound. Invite them to act out words like *saw* and *pause*.

"We have two new vowel teams to learn today! That means we'll almost have our toolbox filled up, and that means we'll *almost* be ready to help Rasheed!"

"Yes!" the class cheered.

"Let's study these new teams so we're ready to use them. I know a snap word that has that *awwww* sound in it!" I wrote the word *saw* on the easel, as kids called out the word. "Right! Let's take a closer look at it. Hmm, . . . I see a new vowel team." I underlined the *AW* in the word.

"Now let me listen for the sound this vowel team is making. *Sawwwwww*. It's the same sound I made earlier in my story! Say it with me and listen for the sound *AW* makes."

"*Sawwwwww*."

"Say the /ô/ sound when I point to this vowel team," I said, pointing under the letters *AW*. "Now let's read this whole word again." I ran my finger under the word *saw* as the class read the word together. Then I used the word in a few sentences to give a bit of context. "I *saw* my sister walk into the school building. I *saw* an airplane high in the sky! Can everyone act that out with me?" We raised a hand to our brow as if we were peering up into the sky.

"Some words use *AW* to make the sound /ô/, but some words use *AU* to make that same /ô/ sound. Let's pretend I wanted to write the word *pause*. I hear a /p/ sound at the beginning." I recorded a *P* on the easel. "Then I hear an /ô/ sound. In this word, *AU* is making that sound." I recorded the vowel team. "And at the end of the word *pause*, there's an *S*. I also know from seeing this word in a book that it has an *E* at the end." I finished writing the word and underlined the vowel team.

"This vowel team *AU* says . . ."

Today's rug time activity asks kids to not only read words, but also act them out. You'll want to incorporate a little drama throughout your teaching and active engagement to set them up for this work today.

"/ô/," the class filled in.

"And this word says . . ."

"*Pause*!" they read as I moved my finger from left to right under the word.

"I pressed *pause* on the remote control," I said, putting the word into a sentence. "Can you act that out with me? I'll be a person on TV and you press *pause*." I pretended to run on the spot and froze as kids raised their remote controls and pointed them at me.

ACTIVE ENGAGEMENT/LINK

Rally children to build some new words with *AW* and *AU*. Ask kids to listen to the words in sentences, say and write the words, act them out, and build new words that are similar.

"Now it's your turn to build some new words with *AW* or *AU*. Does everyone have their materials ready?" I scanned the group, checking to see that everyone had a whiteboard and marker. "Ready to do some construction? Let's start with the word *saw*. You should know this word in a snap!"

As children wrote the word *saw* on their whiteboards, I jotted it down on an index card and placed the card in a pocket chart. "Check that you've spelled it right!" I called out.

"Now see if you can turn *saw* into *claw*. 'My cat scratched the couch with her *claw*.' When you've figured out how to write it, act it out. Can you be a cat scratching something with your claw?" I once again wrote the word on an index card and added it to the pocket chart.

"Can you erase the beginning of *claw* and turn it into *hawk*? Say it slowly to help you. *Hawwwwk*." As students attempted to solve the word, I once again wrote it on an index card and added it to the pocket chart, so they could check their work. "Here's a sentence using *hawk*: 'A *hawk* is a bird with huge wings, similar to an eagle.' Everybody, stretch your wings out and be a hawk!

"Now let's try a word with *AU* in it. Remember, this vowel team also makes an /ô/ sound. Erase all the letters off your board except the *H*. Now write *A, U, L* after it. Turn and talk to your partner. What do you think this word says?" I gave students a moment to try to solve the word. "Yes! Some of you figured out that this says *haul*. It means to work hard at lifting or moving something. 'I had to *haul* my heavy bag all the way to school!'

"Here's the last word! Can you take *haul* and turn it into *fault*? Say it slowly to figure it out! This word also has an *AU* in it. 'It's my fault the milkshake spilled,'" I said, shaking my head sadly and pointing at myself. As students worked on writing the word, I added another card to the pocket chart.

FIG. 15–1 A student turns *saw* into *claw*.

Make sure to remind children to say the words to themselves as they write them down. You'll want to make sure they are the ones doing this job and not you, to support the transfer of this work to their independent writing.

RUG TIME CLUBS

Rally rug clubs to play a game with *AW* and *AU* words. Partners can act out a word, then clubmates can try to guess it.

"You've had a chance to write words with *AW* or *AU*. Now let's try reading some! Let's play a game. You're going to need some room to do this, so pass your boards and markers to the ends of your rows to put them away.

"I'm going to give each rug club a baggie of words. All of these words have *AW* or *AU* in them. You are going to be on a team with your partner. One partnership is going to pull a word out of the baggie. Don't let the other people in your rug club see your word. Really quickly, work with your partner to read the word. Then stand up and act it out! Everybody else in your club needs to try to guess the word. If they don't get it right away, give them a clue, like maybe telling them what letter it starts with. Your rug club can have three guesses before you show them the card and let them read the word. Then the next partnership can pick a word and act it out."

I passed each club a baggie of words, encouraging them to get started right away. Soon the class was full of babies *crawling*, rockets *launching*, and artists *drawing*.

Some of these words will be challenging for your readers, which is why you will want children to be working in partnerships. Make sure that students learning English are in a supportive partnership with someone to help them understand the meaning of each of these words. This activity is a fun way to not only practice decoding words with vowel teams, but also develop new vocabulary.

You can easily differentiate this activity for different rug clubs by selecting specific words for certain groups. For example, if you have some very strong readers in your room, you may want to put together a baggie that includes words like astronaut, daughter, autograph, *and* somersault.

POSSIBLE COACHING MOVES

▸ "Remember, that vowel team says /ô/. Try it again and when you get to that part, say /ô/."

▸ "Yes! That word says *launch*. *Launch* means to shoot up into the sky, like a rocket ship going into space. Do you think you could act that out?"

▸ "Do you see an ending on that word? Take it off. Read the rest. Now add the ending back on."

SHARE • Reviewing *AW* and *AU* Sounds in Words

Remind students how it's important to look carefully at vowel teams when they're figuring out words.

"What fun you had acting out those words! You sure realized how important it was to look carefully and pay attention to the vowel teams." I placed the word card *launch*, from one of the rug clubs' baggies, under the document camera.

"For example, some kids might look at this word quickly and say 'Oh, that says *lunch*.' But if you look carefully you'll spot *AU* in the middle, making an /ô/ sound. That means this word isn't *lunch*, it's *launch*! To *launch* means to shoot up into the sky like a rocket ship, and that's *totally* different from someone eating their *lunch*!"

The class giggled.

"You'll definitely have to look out for these vowel teams when you read tricky words. And remember, when you want to try writing words with the /ô/ sound, sometimes you'll need *AW* and other times you'll need *AU*. You can try it both ways and decide which one looks right."

Add *AW* and *AU* to the linking chart.

"We've learned two new vowel teams today, so let's add them to our chart." I wrote the vowel teams *AW* and *AU* in the next two boxes on the chart.

"Which words would be helpful to remind us of the sounds these two teams make? Turn and talk to your partner. Think about all the words you were reading and writing today."

"I heard so many great ideas! I'm going to pick *claw* to add to our tool for *AW*. Can you take out your magic notebooks," I said, holding up one of my hands like a pretend notebook, "and a magic pen?" I held out the index finger on my other hand as if it was a pen. "First draw a picture, then write the word *claw*. Say it slowly to help you." As students worked I invited one child up to help me write the word on our chart, filling in the vowel team, and drawing a quick illustration. Then we added *faucet*, to provide an anchor for *AU* on the linking chart.

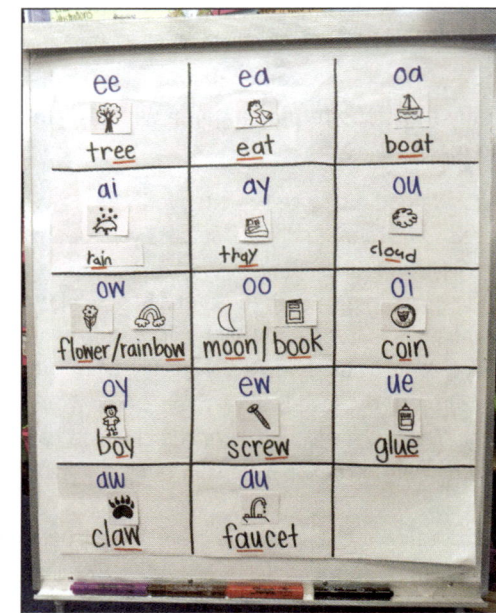

FIG. 15–2 Adding *AW* and *AU* to the chart.

EXTENSION 1 • Making *Because* into a Snap Word and Adding It to the Word Wall

 GETTING READY

- Be ready to show a snap word card for *be* and a word card for a new snap word, *because*.
- Display the "Make it a SNAP word!" anchor chart.

Guide students to reuse the snap word *be* to help build a new snap word, *because*.

"Word builders, I know most of the time when construction workers build a new building they use lots of new materials. They get brand-new nails and boards and get to work. But sometimes construction workers end up using old materials to build new things. They see materials that could be used again in a new way—like maybe a door from an old house can be repainted and reused in a new house.

"This got me thinking. Could we do the same thing with old word wall words? Could old words be reused to help build new words? Let's give it a try."

I held up an old snap word, *be*. "You know the word *be*. What if I wanted to reuse it and build a new word like this one?" I held up the word *because*. "The old word *be* can help me build the first syllable." We clapped *be-cause* together to isolate the first syllable. "And our new vowel team *AU* can help us with the second syllable." We clapped the two syllables in *be-cause* again, this time emphasizing the second one.

"Before adding *because* to the word wall, let's practice it one more time using the 'Make it a SNAP word!' chart."

Together, we went through each step before adding *because* to the class word wall.

EXTENSION 2 • Making Snap Word Sentences

 GETTING READY
- Display snap word cards sets of three on the easel.

Rally students to compose a variety of sentences with snap words they had learned in earlier sessions.

"Grab your whiteboards and markers and meet me at the rug." When students had gathered, I said, "Writers, snap words can help you write more and more during writing workshop. As a way to practice, I thought you and your partner could play a little game. You can take a set of snap words and combine them in different ways to make sentences." I placed three word cards for *about*, *away*, and *two* on the easel. "I could put these words together in a sentence. I could write: 'I am about two stops away from the beach on the train.' or 'She will be away on a trip for about two days.'"

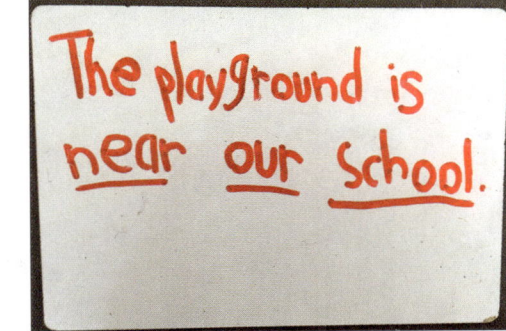

FIG. 15–3 Using snap words to write sentences.

SESSION 15: ADDING TO OUR TOOLBOX: VOWEL TEAMS *AW* AND *AU*

I placed another group of word cards on the easel: *because*, *need*, and *wait*. "Can you think of a way to put these words together in a sentence? You could also make a different kind of sentence, like a question."

I listened while students talked, and after a bit, I said, "I heard a lot of great sentences. Here's one: 'I need to wait for my sister because we walk home together.' I think you're ready to play with your partner.

"Here's another set of snap words. Read the words with your partner and make a sentence. Then write the sentence on your whiteboard. As you write, try not to peek at the snap words! Try to remember what they look like in your mind.

"Once you're both done writing, switch boards and give each other a check-up. You can ask, 'Did my partner spell the snap words correctly? Check! Did my partner use a capital letter to begin the sentence? Check! Do I see punctuation at the end of the sentence? Check!'"

Partners made sentences using the words *near*, *our*, and *school*, and then again using the words *easy*, *know*, and *house*.

These sets of snap words are just examples of the words you might use with your class. You'll want to choose the high-frequency words your kids would benefit from practicing.

SESSION 16

Learning New Snap Words and Making New Words with *IGH*

IN THIS SESSION

TODAY YOU'LL teach students that letters can work in groups of three and the *IGH* team makes the long-vowel sound /ī/. You'll demonstrate by reading the word *high* in a sentence. Point out that by making *high* into a snap word, they can now solve any *IGH* word.

TODAY YOUR STUDENTS will make *high* into a snap word and come to understand how they can now make other *IGH* words, such as *might*, into snap words. Expect children to use what they know about blends and digraphs and common word endings to build new *IGH* words, such as *fighting*, *mighty*, or *bright*.

MINILESSON

CONNECTION

Reintroduce a few familiar stories, such as *Goldilocks and the Three Bears*, that refer to three characters in the title.

I sat in the meeting area with a few books in my lap, as the class settled in their spots. "I bet you all know the story of *Goldilocks and the Three Bears*. And I know in kindergarten, you read this one." I held up a copy of *The Three Billy Goats Gruff*, as children called out the title. Then, I held up a third book. "Here's one of my favorites! *The Three Little Pigs*!

"You might be wondering why I'm talking about fairy tales during phonics workshop. There's something special about stories like these. The characters often work together in groups of three . . . three bears, three billy goats . . . and wait, how many pigs?" I coaxed.

"Three!" the class called back.

"Yes! Three pigs! These stories remind me of letters that work together in the same kind of way."

GETTING READY

✓ Collect a few familiar books that refer to three characters in the title, such as *Goldilocks and the Three Bears*.

✓ Before class, write sentence strips: "I jumped as high as I could on the trampoline." "I think it might rain today, so I'll bring an umbrella just in case." Display each sentence strip on an easel.

✓ Have ready word cards for *high* and *might* to add to your word wall.

✓ Display the "Make it a SNAP word!" anchor chart.

✓ Be sure students have whiteboards and markers.

✓ Display "ABC," "Blends and Digraphs," and "Common Word Endings" charts.

✓ Be ready to add *IGH* to the "Vowel Teams" chart.

PHONICS INSTRUCTION

Phonological Awareness
- Change the beginning, ending, or middle phoneme to make a new word.
- Hear, say, clap, and identify syllables.

Phonics
- Recognize and use letter combinations that represent unique vowel sounds to build and decode words with an *IGH* pattern.

Word Knowledge/Solving
- Use knowledge of vowel patterns as well as digraphs, blends, and inflected endings to write words.

High-Frequency Words
- Learn two new words: *high*, *might*.

♣ **Name the teaching point.**

"Today I want to teach you that letters can work in groups of three. *I*, *G*, and *H* team up to make the long-vowel sound /ī/."

TEACHING

Demonstrate how to use *IGH* to read the word *high* in a sentence.

"Watch how I use *IGH* to read a word. When I see that part in the middle or at the end of word, I can remember that these three letters work together to make the long-vowel sound /ī/." I taped a sentence strip to the easel. Then, reading aloud, I paused before the word *high*.

I jumped as . . .

"Hmm, . . . this word starts with an *H* and makes the /h/ sound. Then, I see the vowel team *IGH*, which makes the sound /ī/. Let me put those parts together. /H//ī/, *high*!" I reread the line, putting the whole sentence together:

I jumped as high as I could on the trampoline.

I quickly wrote the letters *IGH* on the easel, under the word *high*. "Say /ī/ when I point to this vowel team," I said, pointing under the letters *IGH*. "Now let's read this word again." I ran my finger under the word *high* as the class read the word together.

high

igh

Then, I highlighted the vowel team on the printed word card. "Before we add this word to our word wall let's make it a snap word, so we'll remember not just how to read *this* one word, but how to solve *any* word with these three letters, *IGH*." I gestured to the "Make it a SNAP word!" anchor chart.

We went on to study the word, as the class pointed out that the *G* and *H* were silent in the vowel team, comparing it to silent *E*. "You're right. We don't hear the *G* and *H* sounds. The *I*, *G*, and *H* are all working together to make the /ī/ sound." Then, I channeled the group to chant the letters and fill up their whiteboards to practice spelling the word *high* again and again.

Finally, I prompted partners to share a few sentences using the word *high*. I listened for any confusion between *high* and *hi* as partners talked, before sharing back a few examples to help cement meaning.

We are defining "vowel team" as any group of letters that team up to make a vowel sound. Even though IGH contains the consonants G and H, IGH together makes a long I sound, so it's considered to be a vowel team. Similarly, OW and EW are vowel teams because they make vowel sounds.

ACTIVE ENGAGEMENT/LINK

Channel partners to use what they learned about *IGH* and make *might* into a snap word.

"I bet you and your partner could use what you know about these three letters *IGH* to not just read this next word, but to also make it a snap word!" I taped a new sentence strip to the easel:

I think it might rain today, so I'll bring an umbrella just in case.

"Work together to read this sentence and then follow the steps to turn this word," I tapped the word *might*, which I had underlined, "into a snap word, so we can add it to our word wall."

As partners worked together, I listened in, coaching children as they studied, spelled, and wrote the word *might* on their whiteboards.

RUG TIME CLUBS

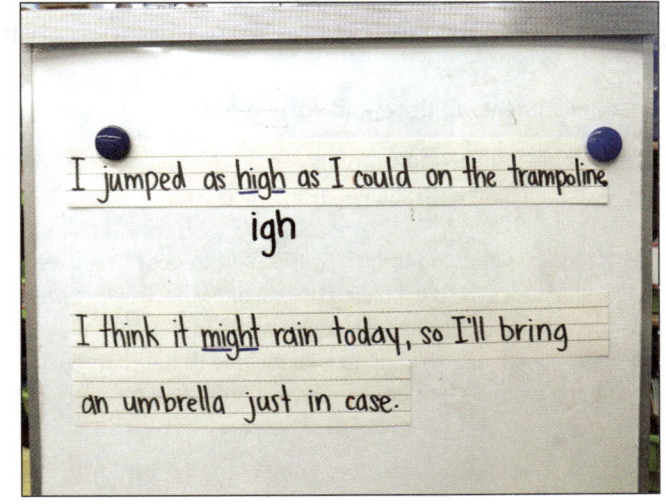

FIG. 16–1 Sentences with new snap words containing *IGH*.

Rally rug clubs to use *IGH* and words like *high* and *might* to build new words.

"Wow! You didn't just read *might*. You turned it into a snap word." I snapped my fingers. "I wonder if you'll be able to use *IGH* and words like *high* and *might* to build a truckload of new words. What do you think? Are you up for the challenge?" The kids quickly agreed.

I displayed the "ABC," "Blends and Digraphs," and "Common Word Endings" charts from earlier units. "These charts can help you try out new beginnings and endings to build new words. You can take *might* and add a new beginning or ending and listen for a real word. Then, you can write the new word on your board and check that it looks right. Work with your club to build as many words as you can!" I sang out, "Let's go, let's go. It's time to work. Let's go!"

I moved around the rug as clubs worked together, coaching in, as needed.

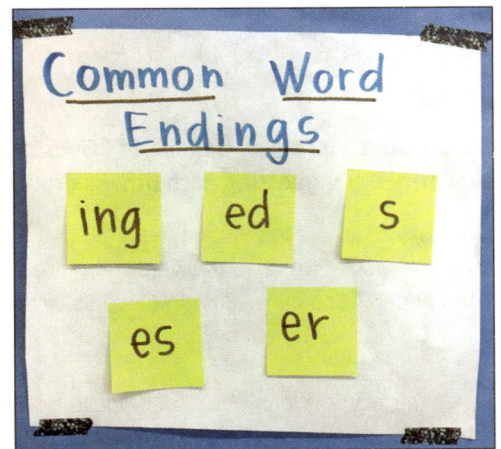

> ### POSSIBLE COACHING MOVES
>
> ▸ "It helps to move through the letters on the 'ABC' chart, listening for a real word. Then, write it and check if it looks right. *Bight* sounds like a real word, but it's spelled a different way. Try again!"
>
> ▸ "Can you add an ending you know? Add *-ing* to *fight*. What word do you have? Now try another ending, like *-er* or *-s*."
>
> ▸ "Use the 'Blends and Digraphs' chart. Put a blend on the front of *IGH*. What words can you build?"

SESSION 16: LEARNING NEW SNAP WORDS AND MAKING NEW WORDS WITH *IGH*

SHARE • Adding *IGH* to Your Linking Chart

Channel students to draw and write the *IGH* word *light* to add to the "Vowel Teams" chart.

"You've built so many words with these three letters, *IGH*! When I point to you, read aloud just one of your new words." I quickly pointed to each student as they called out a word with the new vowel team, sometimes repeating one another.

"Sensational! I'm going to pick *light* to add to our 'Vowel Teams' chart for our final box, *IGH*. Can you take out your magic notebooks," I said, holding up one of my hands like a pretend notebook, "and a magic pen?" I held out the index finger on my other hand as if it was a pen. "First draw a picture, then write the word *light*. Say it slowly." As students worked, I invited one child up to help me add to the chart by filling in the vowel team, drawing a quick illustration, and writing the word *light* to provide an anchor for *IGH* on the linking chart.

EXTENSION 1 • Guess My Rule

GETTING READY

- Make sure each partnership has a small copy of the word wall, a whiteboard, and a marker.
- Take the word cards for *about*, *down*, and *house* from the word wall and put them on the easel.

Set partners up to play a game of "Guess My Rule," in which they take turns grouping words according to similarities and guessing each other's grouping rules.

I invited kids to the rug, asking them to bring their personal word walls and a whiteboard and marker. "We've added quite a few snap words to the word wall since we last played 'Guess My Rule.' Do you remember how to play?" A few kids nodded. "You make a group of words by thinking about what's the same about all the words in the group. That is the rule. And then others try to guess your rule. Let's have one try together."

I took the words *about*, *down*, and *house* from the word wall and placed them on the easel. "Look really close. Say them out loud so you can listen to the sounds. How are they the same? Don't shout out! Keep the rule in your head so everyone can think. When you are ready to guess my rule, put a thumb on your knee."

After a few moments I said, "Okay, turn and tell your partner what my rule is. How are they the same?" I heard some say, "They all make the vowel sound /ou/!"

"Yes!" I said. "They all have a vowel team making the sound /ou/. The vowel teams are *OW* and *OU*. Let's try another one." I took out the words *two* and *who*. Kids talked with their partners about how both words had three letters and ended with the sound /o͞o/.

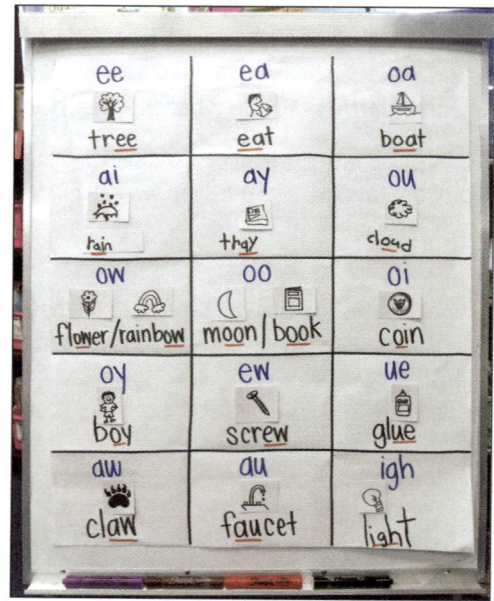

FIG. 16–2 Adding one last vowel team to the class linking chart.

"You've got it!" I said. "Many of you noticed two rules. Ready to play with your partner? Take out your personal word wall and search for two or three words that fit a rule. Remember a rule can be:

- "a number of letters
- "beginning sounds
- "ending sounds
- "vowel or vowel team sounds
- "parts that look the same (*day*, *play*)

"Write the words that fit your rule on your whiteboard. When both partners are ready, switch boards and try to guess each other's rule. Play a few rounds and see if you can get faster at spotting the rule."

EXTENSION 2 • Listening for Syllables

GETTING READY

- Think of many single- and multisyllabic words that you could call out to students to tap, clap, or snap syllables.

Invite students to tap, clap, or snap syllables in words.

"Watch and listen and then repeat after me," I signaled the class. I snapped my fingers twice. The class followed suit. I tapped my foot on the ground three times and again the class repeated. Finally, I clapped once. "All this tapping, clapping, and snapping has got me thinking about syllables. When your table lines up for lunch today, I'll call out a word. Say the word and then tap, clap, or snap the number of syllables you hear as you make your way into line. Let's practice together." I called out the word *higher*. "*High-er*," kids called back, and everyone indicated two syllables with a tap, clap, or snap. I continued calling out a word to each table, alternating between single- and multisyllabic words.

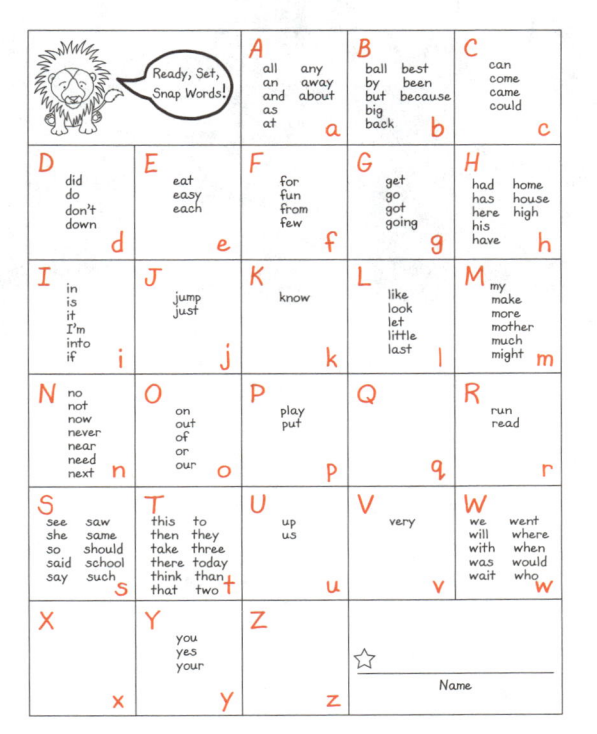

FIG. 16–3   A personal word wall.

SESSION 16: LEARNING NEW SNAP WORDS AND MAKING NEW WORDS WITH *IGH*   **109**

SESSION 17

Building Vowel Town
A Celebration

GETTING READY

- ✓ Prepare a roll of drawing paper with a banner written across the top, "Welcome to Vowel Town!" and hide it behind the easel.
- ✓ Print out Rasheed's Blueprint No. 1 for yourself. Be ready to display it and add labels to the images on the blueprint.
- ✓ Print out six different blueprints, one for each rug club.
- ✓ Position Rasheed in the meeting area beside a pile of rolled-up blueprints.
- ✓ Gather glue sticks, construction paper, tape, scissors, and markers for each rug club. Make sure students also have their whiteboards.
- ✓ Display your "Vowel Teams" chart.
- ✓ Clip the lyrics to the "Word Builder Song" to an easel.

PHONICS INSTRUCTION

Phonological Awareness
- Isolate and pronounce initial, medial vowel, and ending sounds in spoken single-syllable and multisyllabic words.

Phonics
- Recognize and use letter combinations that represent unique vowel sounds to build and decode words.

Word Knowledge/Solving
- Use knowledge of vowel patterns as well as digraphs, blends, and inflected endings to decode and write words.
- Read and take apart simple compound words.

IN THIS SESSION

TODAY YOU'LL help students celebrate all they've learned in this unit. Together, you'll build a map of Vowel Town, a place full of words with vowel teams.

TODAY YOUR STUDENTS will review the vowel teams, sounds, and words on the class linking chart. Expect them to solve blueprint words and to draw and label each word using their knowledge of vowel teams and word parts. They will add their words and drawings to the class map of Vowel Town.

MINILESSON

CONNECTION

Announce Rasheed's big news to your students. He wants to share some building plans, so they can build something really big together—a whole town!

I positioned the class mascot in the meeting area beside a pile of rolled-up blueprints. Then, I called out to the class with urgency, "Word builders, report to the rug on the double!" I ushered the students to their spots. "Rasheed has big news! He is excited to announce that you are now ready for a very big job, and he has a bunch of building plans to share with you!" I held up one of the blueprints as the kids cheered.

Then, I turned to the lion. "Rasheed, what are we going to build? Are we going to build a table? Something bigger? A bookshelf! Bigger than that? A house! Even bigger?" Kids shouted out guesses.

I pulled out a large roll of drawing paper from behind the easel and recruited one of the students to help me as we unrolled the long sheet, revealing a banner written across the top. We read it aloud, "Welcome to Vowel Town!" Then, I quickly taped the paper down on the tiled floor where I had cleared a space for kids to work.

"Rasheed! We are going to build a whole town? Wow, you weren't kidding. That *is* a very big job! Wait, there's something else we need to know?" I leaned closer to the lion as if to listen. "How terrific!"

Then, I turned back to the class. "Readers and writers, this is turning out to be a very special construction project. You see, you won't use wood and nails to build this town . . . you'll build this town with words!"

❋ **Name the teaching point.**

"Today I want to remind you that word builders gather up all their tools and all their parts to get the job done. You can look and listen for parts you know, like vowel teams, to solve enough words to fill a whole town!"

TEACHING

Channel children to check their "supplies" for the big project. Review all the vowel teams, sounds, and words on the "Vowel Teams" chart.

"Word builders, it's time to get to work! Before a construction crew starts working, they stop and check that they have everything they need. 'Nails?' they ask. 'Check! Hammers? Check! Boards? Check!'

"Let's check our supplies. You've learned so much about vowel teams. Let's take stock of everything we know before we begin this big project!" Pretending to act like the foreman on a work crew, I called out the first vowel team. "*EE*?" I asked, pointing to our linking chart.

"Check!" the class responded. Then we read that part of the chart together. "/ē/, *tree*!" We continued in this manner reading each vowel team together and reviewing the sounds they make.

ACTIVE ENGAGEMENT/LINK

Guide students to study the word *roads* on the blueprint. Demonstrate drawing and spelling the words *roads* and *train tracks*. Then ask partners to read and write the next pair of words.

"If we are ever going to build a whole town, we'd better get going! Builders use blueprints to figure out what goes where. Let's consult Rasheed's plans to learn what we need to build." I pulled out the plan labeled *Blueprint No. 1*. "Rasheed has laid out exactly what Vowel Town will need. Let's read these pictures and words, looking and listening for parts we know, especially vowel teams!"

I placed the blueprint on the document camera. "Hmm, . . . take a close look at this word." I slid my finger under the word *roads*. "Rrrrrrr . . . I spy a vowel team in the middle, *OA*, /ō/, like *boat*." I pointed to the linking chart. "/R//ō//d/ . . . *roads*! Of course, our town needs roads!" I picked up a black marker and quickly drew a long winding road across the paper. Then, I asked the class to help me spell the word as I labeled the drawing. "*R-O-A-D-S.*"

SESSION 17: BUILDING VOWEL TOWN

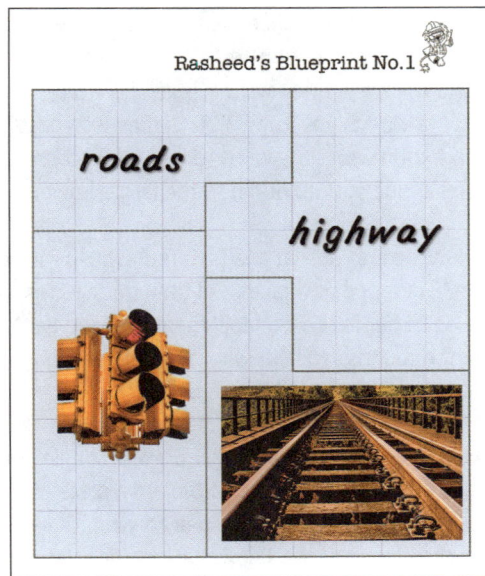

FIG. 17–1 The first of seven blueprints for Vowel Town.

This choral reading of the class linking chart allows students to both reinforce and consolidate their learning of vowel teams across the unit.

You'll notice that each "blueprint" gives students an opportunity to use vowel teams to both read and write new words.

Try to keep this demonstration fast and focused to allow enough time for students to practice this work in partnerships, and then in clubs.

"Hmm, . . . I'm thinking we could add even more words to our town. Let's add a street sign to this road. Let's call this 'Main Street.' What parts will we need to write it? Say the words *main . . . street . . .* Do you hear any parts you know?" Together, we consulted the "Vowel Teams" chart and I wrote the words on a strip of construction paper and quickly used a glue stick to add it to the large drawing.

"Now take a look at the picture Rasheed included here. What do you see?" I tapped on a picture of train tracks. "Yes, train tracks! We can add those to our town and label them. Will you work with a partner to listen for the sounds you hear when you say the words *train tracks*? Then, write the words on your whiteboards."

As children worked, I quickly drew a simple train track pattern across one part of the town. Then, I clipped a piece of construction paper to the easel and asked for a volunteer to write the words, as we listened and checked for parts we knew. I asked the student to glue the words *train tracks* to the map.

FIG. 17–2 Students use words with vowel teams to build a large-scale map of Vowel Town.

"Now check the blueprint to find out what else we need to build. Work together to read the printed word and to spell the word in the picture. Make sure to look out and listen up for vowel teams! You can use our chart to help you remember the sounds they usually make." I coached kids as they worked to read and write the second pair of words.

After a minute or so, I called the group back together. "So it sounds like this town will also need things like," I gestured for the class to join me in reading the remaining words on the blueprint, "a *highway* and a *traffic light*. I'll add those to our map, but while I do that, Rasheed has blueprints for each rug club to build the rest of Vowel Town!"

You might want to plan out the roads, train tracks, and highway ahead of time to move through this part of the lesson quickly.

RUG TIME CLUBS

Rally children to work together to solve their blueprint words and to draw and label each word, using their knowledge of vowel teams and word parts. Then ask them to add their words and drawings to the class map of Vowel Town.

I held up a set of six different blueprints, one for each rug club. "Each group will have a special blueprint with words you'll need to read and write to build another section of Vowel Town. Work together to solve these words. Then, you can use markers and construction paper to draw and label each word! You might even think about *more* words to add. If you're not sure which vowel team to use, you can write the word on your whiteboard, trying it a few ways, before deciding which word looks right."

You may choose to plan out the roads, train tracks, and highway ahead of time to move through this part of the lesson quickly.

FIG. 17–2 *continued*

I instructed the class to spread out across the room to give each other more space to work. As kids did so, we sang, "Let's go, let's go. It's time to work. Let's go . . ." Then, I distributed a blueprint and colored paper, glue sticks, tape, scissors, and markers to each club. I suggested that students first write the word, then draw the picture around it before adding it to the class map.

As children worked to read and spell words, featuring vowel teams, such as *lighthouse*, *mountain*, *restaurant*, *sheep*, *goats*, and *playground*, I coached them to use the linking chart to look and listen for parts they had learned. I voiced over to the class, encouraging each word builder to draw and write one of the words on the blueprint to get it ready to add to the class map of Vowel Town. As children completed their drawings and labels, I invited them to glue it to the large sheet of drawing paper, creating a collage of pictures and words.

SHARE • Celebrating Vowel Town

Commend your students for using all they've learned about vowel teams and word parts to build Vowel Town. Convey Rasheed's message that they'll be word builders forever and ever!

I directed the class to clean up all of their building materials and return to the meeting area. I pulled the large map off the floor and taped it across one wall of the classroom so the class could marvel at their creation.

"Word builders, I bet you are feeling very proud! I know I am! You worked so hard to use all the word parts you know to read and write lots and lots of words . . . enough to fill a whole town!" I stood beside the map. "You built a bookstore, and a restaurant, and a school, and houses." I pointed to each part of the map. "You even added more words than Rasheed gave you, like this sign outside the restaurant, 'Eat good food right now!' Check out all those vowel teams!"

I sat back in my chair at the head of the meeting area and picked up the class lion. "Today is the last day of our unit, but Rasheed wants you to know that you'll be a word builder forever and ever! You can build new words with parts you know, like vowel teams, to get the job done whenever you read and write! Let's sing our 'Word Builder Song' together to celebrate how much we've learned!" I clipped the lyrics to the easel and we sang to commemorate the end of the unit.

FIG. 17–3   A completed map of Vowel Town.